About Man and God and Law

ADVANCE PRAISE

"An evocative, learned, and personal analysis of a carefully curated collection of Dylan songs. A capacious and soulful book."

—**Dana Spiotta**, author of *Wayward*, *Stone Arabia*, and *Eat the Document*

"Most theory about rock music flattens the dangerous God-intoxicated spirit that powers its heart, but Stephen Arnoff's brilliant excavating of Bob Dylan's soul is like watching Orpheus descend into the underworld. Arnoff is not just a critic. He shows us not only why Dylan is essential, but why Dylan matters to what matters most: Holiness is not a state, but a struggle, a wrestling with God and each other. Arnoff's book is a revelation about Dylan, music, and how they both get us closer to the ideal."

—**Peter Bebergal**, author of *Season of the Witch* and *Strange Frequencies*

"Stephen Arnoff's *About Man and God and Law* is a stirring meditation on the cosmic dimensions of Bob Dylan's storied body of work, reminding readers that this is music that is ultimately greater than the sum of its parts. Arnoff invites you to lean along with him into the philosophical iridescence and theological catharsis at the heart of Dylan's oeuvre, showing us the reasons why geniuses from Nina and Jimi to Odetta and Sam Cooke had dazzling conversations with his words and sounds. A journey in enchantment."

—**Daphne Brooks**, author of *Liner Notes for the Revolution: The Intellectual Life of Black Feminist Sound* and William R. Kenan, Jr. Professor of African American Studies, American Studies, Women's, Gender, and Sexuality Studies, and Music, Yale University

"Arnoff takes us on a startlingly original journey into the mystery of Bob Dylan, the legend we thought we knew. Arnoff sets the bard against the widest backdrop: Greek myth and rock 'n' roll, Romantic poets and Talmudic rabbis, prophets and iconoclasts, Homer and Chuck Berry, Walt Whitman and Little Richard, John Brown and Nina Simone. Arnoff's writing moves from careful argument to poetic exuberance, from historical erudition to hypnotic stream of consciousness. In both style and cultural reach, Arnoff's book is not just *about* Dylan, it is itself Dylanesque. Arnoff makes us experience Dylan as the 'solitary seeker' who has always 'bargained for salvation'—but also as our era's troubadour who boldly proclaims the truth amidst the ruins of the 'United States of Pompeii.'"

—**Nathaniel Berman**, Rahel Varnhagen Professor in
Religious Studies, Brown University

"In this time of global unrest and accelerating change, Arnoff reawakens us to the enduring power of poetry and music to speak to the soul's deepest questions. His exploration of Dylan's work moves us into the hidden spaces of our innermost vulnerabilities: 'Why are we here?' 'Who are we?' And in Dylan's own words: 'How does it feel?' Dylan's query notably echoes the equally salient question so often posed by the iconic civil rights leader Ruby Sales: 'Where does it hurt?' Both Dylan and Sales understand that we must go straight to the heart's core in order to seek truth. In this book, Arnoff takes us alongside Dylan's own journey to answer these questions, using Dylan's songs to explore the artist's lifelong pilgrimage; a pilgrimage that leads him, ultimately, to a place of humility and acceptance as he realizes there is so much that we cannot ever really know. This book reminds us that we do not ever walk this way alone. Through the music, we too are traveling with Dylan, and the Spirit is blowing where it will, bringing with her wisdom that is simultaneously timeless and ever new. In an era when more and more respondents to polling list their religious affiliation as 'none,' Dylan and Arnoff offer us a musical and poetic roadmap to real salvation: the awakening of empathy for ourselves and for those who walk beside us on the long odyssey of being human in an ever-changing, chaotic world."

—**Rev. Posey Krakowsky**, Church of the Ascension, New York, NY

"This is not just another bio book about a musical giant. In stunningly stylish prose, Stephen Arnoff offers up much more than a hymn of praise to Bob Dylan and his contribution to 20th century American music. Arnoff quickly commands our immediate attention, but does so as if he were gently strumming a weeping guitar. He probes the search of every artist, himself included—to solve the enigma of his own being on creative and spiritual levels. The entire work reveals the struggle of every great artist to raise the quality of his own self-expression and to find release and liberation—much more than a mere codification and chronicle of the works of an artist. The book is also a philosophical text. Arnoff draws us in in a most intimate fashion to share a process that defines the quality of artistry that not only shows us the path of Bob Dylan, but it gives us a view of our own doom and blessing if we dare to obey the inner drive to communicate with the world outside ourselves."

—**Michael Lutin**, world-renowned astrologer, former *Vanity Fair* columnist, and author of *Humans Rising* and *The Art and Magic of Astrological Interpretation*

"A devoted and expert fan's reflections on the spiritual spaces Bob Dylan has filled in the hearts of many of us. Stephen Arnoff's *About Man and God and Law* is a lively and personal take on some of the fundamental themes that the songwriter has engaged across his career."

—**Richard Thomas**, author of *Why Dylan Matters* and George Martin Lane Professor of Classics at Harvard University

"'I ain't no false prophet,' claims Bob Dylan on his most recent album, and, in its entirety, Stephen Arnoff's *About Man and God and Law: A Guide to Bob Dylan's Spiritual Wisdom* demonstrates exactly how Dylan is the ultimate 'enemy of the unlived meaningless life.' As widely read as his subject, Arnoff sets out succinct readings of Dylan's body of work and positions the songs and their creator in relevant cultural contexts, connecting the work to the thinkers and situations that inspired it. With its continued focus on Dylan's expressions of the human condition in the light of God and law, in chapters that range from 'Salvation' to 'Love' to 'Death,' this text makes clear the redemptive power of Dylan's songs. Broadly imagined and eminently readable, Arnoff's analyses uncover Dylan's music as an ongoing expression of spiritual sustenance."

—**Roxanne Harde**, editor (with Irvin Streight) of *Reading the Boss: Interdisciplinary Approaches to the Works of Bruce Springsteen*

"A lively journey through Bob Dylan's work via wide-ranging riffs on Dylan's untiring searches for meaning. From Hebrew prophets to ancient Roman theology, from Dante to Biggie Smalls, Arnoff frames Dylan's storied restlessness in an eclectic narrative of how *spirituality* and *wisdom* may be viable right here, right now. Nonreligious Dylan fans will find valuable insights into individual songs, and a grounded commitment to both the playfulness and gravitas of Bob Dylan's art."

—**Nina Goss**, author of *Tearing the World Apart: Bob Dylan and the Twenty-First Century*

"Can we separate the myth and the reality of Bob Dylan? Should we even try? A question for the ages and one that will be debated for eons. Without doubt, the rock n' roll Nobel Laureate is a bit of both. Did he design it that way? Was it divine intervention, is he a freewheelin' *Deus ex machina*? Or was it just us, his fans, heaping this robe of responsibility on him? Big questions. Dr. Stephen Arnoff digs deep to find answers—and may actually discover more questions—about the man and the myth. It's a trail others have followed to varying success, but Arnoff has discovered fresh territory. I loved following his journey, chasing the image of Dylan in his 60+ years of creating higher pop art. This is not the usual music related book about a great artist and his life. It is so much more. An excellent and thought provoking read, and a must have for any Dylanologist!"

—**Christian Swain**, Host of the Rock N Roll
Archaeology Podcast

"Using one line from Dylan's 1965 song 'Maggie's Farm' and three words in particular—man, God, and law—as the foundation, Arnoff extrapolates on the iconic singer's musical past and musical present as well as his musical and spiritual legacy. In these very readable pages, Whitman, Guthrie, Springsteen, and Kerouac meet sacred texts, the myth of America, and the notion of self-invention and self-creation. By exploring the entirety of the Dylan canon thematically, the author has fashioned an erudite and thoughtful meditation on salvation and faith and what makes a life meaningful as seen through the prism of Mr. Dylan's words and many personas. For spiritual seekers and Dylan fans alike."

—**June Skinner Sawyers**, co-editor of *Long Walk Home:
Reflections on Bruce Springsteen*

About Man & God & Law

The Spiritual Wisdom of BOB DYLAN

STEPHEN DANIEL ARNOFF

NEW YORK

LONDON • NASHVILLE • MELBOURNE • VANCOUVER

About Man & God & Law

The Spiritual Wisdom of Bob Dylan

Published in New York, New York, by Morgan James Publishing. Morgan James is a trademark of Morgan James, LLC. www.MorganJamesPublishing.com

Scriptural verses from the Hebrew Bible (Old Testament) are cited from *The Holy Scriptures: A New Translation* (JPS 1917), copyright © 1985 by JPS.

Scriptural verses from the New Testament are cited from the *Holy Bible, English Standard Version*, copyright © 2016 by Crossway Bibles, a publishing ministry of Good News Publishers.

Proudly distributed by Ingram Publisher Services.

Morgan James BOGO™

A **FREE** ebook edition is available for you or a friend with the purchase of this print book.

CLEARLY SIGN YOUR NAME ABOVE

Instructions to claim your free ebook edition:
1. Visit MorganJamesBOGO.com
2. Sign your name CLEARLY in the space above
3. Complete the form and submit a photo of this entire page
4. You or your friend can download the ebook to your preferred device

ISBN 9781631956881 paperback
ISBN 9781631956898 ebook
Library of Congress Control Number: 2021941342

Cover Design by:
Rachel Lopez
www.r2cdesign.com

Interior Design by:
Chris Treccani
www.3dogcreative.net

Author Photo by:
Sharon Gabay

Morgan James PUBLISHING

Builds with... **Habitat for Humanity** Peninsula and Greater Williamsburg

Morgan James is a proud partner of Habitat for Humanity Peninsula and Greater Williamsburg. Partners in building since 2006.

Get involved today! Visit MorganJamesPublishing.com/giving-back

For my children

Contents

Introduction:

About Man and God and Law

S ing in me, Muse, and through me tell the story.

Here comes another book about Bob Dylan—carved into the layers of rock and roll mythologies and cover-ups, of masters of war and higher planes of human purpose, and of the question posed by Bob Dylan in "Like a Rolling Stone" that defines his era: "How does it feel?"

To be alive, to not know, to be on your own, and to live in someone else's song—how does it feel?

Follow the path of spiritual wisdom over three millennia to the shaman's hut, the priest's sanctuary, or the scholar's study. From Alexandria, Athens, Jerusalem, and Rome to the Cavern Club, the Cafe Wha?, and the Apollo Theater at the dawn of the age of rock and roll, a restless confederation of seekers is trying to make sense of the world. Their shared creed is this: "I'm the enemy of the unlived meaningless life."

That's it, right there in "False Prophet," a song from Bob Dylan's 2020 album *Rough and Rowdy Ways*. For the spiritual seeker, a life that is anything less than a search for meaning is simply a waste of time.

False prophet, man of wisdom, man of peace—Bob Dylan has been holding court in songs about living a meaningful life for six decades, mixing up the medicine of the same traditions and questions about spiritual creativity and curiosity that have moved sages and seers for thousands of years.

Many of our assumptions about spiritual purpose, sensual pleasure, and the essence of work, community, country, race, and the divine have germinated in Bob Dylan's need to know what's blowing in the wind and how it feels. Channeled through his music and persona, Dylan's quest and questions have animated the mandate of a liberation movement called rock and roll.

Bob Dylan has called for popular music to include spiritual contemplation and iconoclasm as well as reverence and awe. Because of the generations of artists and fans that have followed his lead or joined his chorus, popular music has reenchanted and reframed the worries and wonder that have always occupied the religious imagination.

When Bob Dylan overhears Maggie's mother talking "to all the servants about man and God and law" in the 1965 song "Maggie's Farm," he telegraphs a set of themes that flow through his entire body of work. Speculating about this holy, rocking trinity, this kinetic nexus of "man and God and law," Dylan names a theological blues that everybody knows—the need for salvation and the urge for faith despite our troubles.

This book is an expansive interpretation of this single line from "Maggie's Farm" and all that it carries. I will be parsing Dylan's songs like sacred texts, listening as closely as I can to his words and music to glean what they mean, to wonder what they teach and inspire, and to linger with the riddles and questions imbedded within them. As with any set of sacred texts, the art of shaping meaning out of Dylan's canon will require a holistic approach. I take into account the musical and cultural realities that define his era, the history and sociology of religion, and the creative techniques upon which Dylan calls. The result is a guide to Bob Dylan's spiritual wisdom that also reflects upon the possibilities of our own.

Here is how the book plays out more specifically: After charting a map of traditions for seeking salvation and living a life of faith prior to Dylan in chapters 1 and 2, I will focus on each of the three key words Dylan calls out in that verse harvested on "Maggie's Farm." In chapters 3, 4, and 5, "man" opens pathways to salvation through love, the teacher, and death.

Framing these terms precisely—man and God and law—is essential for making for the best, clearest use of them. This is true of the word "man" more than any of the three. When I refer to "man" in context of this passage, I mean "human beings," not just males. So it goes with many of sacred texts I most admire. While they speak words of spiritual truth, they often employ language, style, or intent quite different from my own. This is particularly true when it comes to gender, about which the sensibilities of great sages and artists, including Dylan, can be downright offensive to people affirming feminism and gender justice, which I unequivocally do. There is more about the challenges of gender, sacred text, and rock and roll below and throughout the book.

Chapters 6 and 7 consider "God" as memory and America, two landscapes—text and context, respectively—where Dylan's journeys of salvation take place. I look at "law" in chapter 8, considering through the lens of Dylan's work the systems people can choose to rely upon, abandon, or construct to codify lives of meaning. *About Man and God and Law* concludes with chapter 9, thoughts about where Bob Dylan's musical, spiritual, and intellectual legacy might lead.

There are a few more things you need to know before we begin.

First, have your preferred listening device available as you read. To enjoy this book best is to hear it imbedded in the songs described by the words on the page.

There is also the matter of the teller of the tale—that's me.

After more than three decades of making music, and of thinking, writing, and teaching about it, my testimony for all things musical paraphrases what Bob Dylan once said about freedom of speech: without music, I'd be in the swamp. In other words, I am a music lover just like you, and immersing myself in music, especially the music of Bob Dylan, is a joyous, transformative, comforting, and inspiring spiritual experience by every measure. I hope you will find some of that soulful magic in this book.

I'm also a white male—like so many of the writers and critics who have prophesized with their pens and tried to explain popular music while feeding its myths—in addition to being a scholar of music and religion, born to and living in the Jewish faith. I have my own notions of text and context to sift through to get to truths in Dylan's work that we can learn from together. Certain gifts and burdens color my sensibility and set my limitations. Some are advantageous, some are privileged, and some produce blind spots others will need to illuminate.

Writing about popular music often means getting tangled up in cultural appropriation and white- or male-centric thinking that must be cut through. These are sensitive topics in our day, and rightly so. On the one hand, I am still naive enough to believe that great music has enough that is human and holy within it to be heard no matter who is talking about it, and no matter what we think defines the commentator, fan, or critic on the outside. And on the other hand—really both hands—critique and exploration of music, like music itself, needs to fight against the grain of its biases, especially the ways we underplay and under-hear diversity, which we ignore at the risk of not understanding this music at all.

Restlessness and disappointment about the missed opportunities of rock and roll and religion gnaw at me. Neither Bob Dylan, rock and roll, popular music, nor the great traditions of myth, philosophy, and religion called upon in this book can stake any permanent claim to bringing peace, love, and understanding. But even if the social contracts of the musical and religious realms I know best have edged up to their dates of expiration and obsolescence, I still believe there is a chance to redeem them.

Bob Dylan sang in "Sugar Baby":

> I got my back to the sun 'cause the light is too intense
> I can see what everybody in the world is up against
> You can't turn back—you can't come back, sometimes we push too far
> One day you'll open up your eyes and you'll see where we are

For more than sixty years, experiencing Dylan's songs has been like unfolding a map to the secret, soulful places sages and seers have always longed to go. Through the prism of his vision and the echo of his voice, this guide to Dylan's spiritual wisdom aims to make good on the promise that if we look closely enough at his body of work—precisely at a moment when the world we thought we knew seems like uncharted territory—we can open up our eyes to see not only where we really are, but where we need to go.

Sing in me, Muse, and through me tell the story. Here comes another book about Bob Dylan. Thanks for listening.

Stephen Daniel Arnoff
Jerusalem | August 2021

Man

1. Salvation

I bargained for salvation and they gave me a lethal dose

We live in an age in which a popular musician can be a prophet—changing times made for Bob Dylan just as much as he changed them.

As rock and roll emerged as a cultural force in the 1950s and '60s, much of its audience had already distanced itself from religious practices and ideas honed for thousands of years to sustain, sanctify, and celebrate the ways that man and God and law meet. Even if God may not have left the building entirely—as Elvis was said to have done after his glitzy, over-the-top shows in the 1970s—the possibility of experiencing meaning and purpose with the divine was fading for many of the people who would become popular music's biggest fans and stars. When it came to houses of worship, the people—not God—had left the building.

But new gatherings and congregations, unbound from formal traditions, continued to coalesce around questions about proof of life's ultimate purpose. People still sought transcendence, hungering for comfort beyond what day-to-day experience could provide. The world needed new pathways for feeling and expressing an ancient, irrepressible desire for seeking salvation, that sense of being in the right place at the right time, protected, saved, chosen, at home, and no longer alone.

Bob Dylan's generation of Americans was born in the aftermath of a world war, growing up as America expanded its cultural hegemony exponentially. Raised as mass media came into its own, immersed in the staggered blossoming of emancipation movements of people of color, women, and gays and lesbians, Dylan and his peers embodied the emergence of youth as a new north star of influence and profit in the global marketplace. But what about the prophets and prophecy imbedded in the profit? For this, in stepped rock and roll, preaching salvation through a new economy of rebellion and identity that Bob Dylan would infuse with intellectual rigor as well as wisdom, both of and for the ages and by and for the people.

A great awakening had raised a tent open to all in the center of town as Dylan reached his teens. It was called radio. Rock's first generation—Little Richard, Chuck Berry, Bo Diddley, Buddy Holly, Elvis, and a host of other pioneers—were kicking the tires on a new kind of religion emerging from the missed opportunities of the old ones. American popular music had already been defined by the dialogue between gospel, jazz, blues, country, and folk that circulated between the church, the club, the front porch, and the street corner. Now rock and roll was bringing all of these voices to scale.

Some sixty million viewers watched Elvis on *The Ed Sullivan Show.* That was a third of the country at the time. Many of those viewers were kids like Dylan. "The first Velvet Underground album only sold 10,000 copies," musician and producer Brian Eno once said, "but everyone who bought it formed a band." An entire generation of rockers seems to have a story about wanting to be cool like Elvis, or hearing Little Richard vamp or Chuck Berry shred and feeling every creative synapse ignite. "In my universe, Chuck is irreplaceable," Bob Dylan told *Rolling Stone* in 2009. But what all this creative energy and musical innovation meant and where it would lead remained an open question.

And this was the question posed to Marlon Brando's "Johnny" when he was asked what he was rebelling against in the touchstone 1953 film *The Wild One*, which Dylan and his friends might have known on the cusp of their own teenage years. "What have you got?" was his answer. First-generation rockers like Brando's "Johnny" and Elvis had catchy melodies and a snappy comeback when things got tricky, but like another icon so many future rockers such as Bob Dylan would worship before finding their own respective spotlights, these were still rebels without a cause.

Rapturous rock and roll inspired shouting and shaking as freeing as what you might find at an old-school tent-revival meeting. Such scenes of ecstasy were already familiar to the American landscape in various forms, including the Great Awakenings, Pentecostalism, and all variety of revivals encouraging visceral expression of direct contact with the divine.

Black music emanating from the church in particular was core to rock's essential sound and culture taking shape. Any comprehensive history of American music—any history of America, really—needs to probe and celebrate how profoundly the music of the Black church flowed into the broader culture. Even as I hear that influence here and elsewhere (though admittedly far from exhaustively) it's clear that for those who abandoned religion as their primary spiritual base, there was no mainstream vessel in which to nurture the yearning for transformation and belonging that houses of worship used to fulfill—until music did.

Road Maps for the Soul

Bob Dylan was in the right place at the right time when he arrived in snowbound Manhattan in January 1961, acoustic guitar in hand, a twenty-year-old college dropout. The world was ready for someone to combine the traditional entanglements of man and God and law with the energy of popular music.

A proto-punk with confidence and ambition, a sublime ear for a tune, a poetic heart, and a whole lot of attitude, Dylan was soon offering contrarian takes on just about everything Brando's "Johnny" might have rebelled against: family, society, sex, work, race, and identity itself. By the time he was twenty-five, fronting a variety of musicians including those who would later be known as the Band, and already a folk-music exile just a few years after he had caught the bug of folk and blues himself, Dylan was calling out "road maps for the soul," as he sang in "Tombstone Blues" in 1965. Merely a decade after the release of Bill Haley & His Comets' "Rock Around the Clock" and only nine years after Elvis's first appearance on *The Ed Sullivan Show*, a young man from Hibbing, Minnesota, was defining the spiritual landscape of popular music.

Rock followed the beat of Dylan's intuitions and restlessness, stepping in time with the start-again, stop-again march of those liberation movements, witnessing its assassinations and wars, wrestling with the dilemmas that societal realignment demanded. While it would eventually inform all variety of musical, cultural, and commercial expression, the best of rock questioned and repurposed authority, urged disruption, and documented and celebrated itself in real time with long-playing liturgies for turntables performed by a pantheon of prophets, priests, shamans, and wizards.

Their names were simple at first, just like the names of their fans and followers: Bob and John and Mick and Paul, and soon Jimi and Janis and Sly, and Joni too. But the names of the bands of their life and times revealed an insistence on liberation at the heart of a musical movement: the Doors; the Miracles; the Who; the Temptations; the Grateful Dead; Creedence Clearwater Revival; Black Sabbath; Earth, Wind & Fire; the Clash; Genesis; Journey; the Runaways; the Cure; Nirvana; Destiny's Child.

As it evolved, musical salvation in the rock era could be a kitschy soundtrack for teenagers caught between domesticity and a hard place, like Meat Loaf's "Paradise by the Dashboard Light," or so sweet it could make you sick, as in Mike Reno of Loverboy's and Ann Wilson of Heart's "Almost Paradise." But it also brought forth a mystical ramble at the edge of the world in a certain song by Led Zeppelin about a lady, a stairway, and the mythic mysteries of glitter and gold. It was Joni Mitchell (and then Crosby, Stills, Nash & Young) enshrining the faces of the pilgrims of Woodstock in holy light, or Pete Townshend of the Who hoping to die before he got old and then claiming that every song he ever wrote was actually about Jesus. It was U2's Bono on his knees, at times insufferably so, asking eighty thousand others to join him in prayer, or Aretha Franklin any time she opened her mouth to sing—"using to the highest degree possible the gift that God gave [her] to use"—while mixing images of romantic and divine redemption in a single verse.

Even when it overreaches, and perhaps *especially* when it overreaches, popular music—just like religion—seeks personal and communal transcendence. It mixes this-world grit and world-to-come glitter and gold to expose spiritual needs that have become harder and harder to understand or fulfill for many. Bob Dylan catalyzed much of a still-unfolding metamorphosis in which culture makers and spiritual seekers could discover through popular music the possibilities of their own depths while also embracing something greater than themselves.

This Is Not Elvis

Psychobilly singer Mojo Nixon once wrote a tune called "Elvis Is Everywhere." It's a tongue-in-cheek deification of the King, who seemed to pop up all over the place in the eighties and nineties. Elvis was in people's dreams and tabloid headlines, an impersonator at weddings, lining the sidewalks on Halloween, and pitching used cars on television. *This Is Elvis*, a documentary chasing down Elvis's history, was narrated by an Elvis impersonator as if he was the disembodied King himself. And then—what do you know?—there was Elvis buying a Slurpee at the local 7-Eleven that very same night.

Elvis was a pop culture mythic force documented by fans, journalists, and intellectuals alike, clear evidence of a hunger in the world to meet gods and angels in dreams and oracles just as believers have always sought the divine.

In 1993's "Fight the Power," Chuck D of Public Enemy called out the deification of a white musician who many believe was cynically packaged as the King, when in fact many of the once and future kings and queens of rock and pop were people of color. Mojo Nixon saw Elvis, jokingly of course, as manifest in everyone everywhere.

If we try to glean theological insight from Mojo Nixon's irony while keeping in mind Chuck D's righteous critique of the whitewashing of popular music, Nixon is describing something universal. Flawed and talented, blessed and cursed, and as commodified and racially divisive as he may have been, life-after-death Elvis was just the latest model of the kind of mythic being to whom we have been granting a stage since people first started using language, music, dance, sacrifice, and prayer to communicate with forces beyond themselves.

For fans and followers of popular musicians, who know their songs and personal stories, who cop their styles and points of view, and who follow their practices and weave the songs and visions into the most important moments of their lives, a musician can be just as present and formative as any religious figure in any age, divine or human, living or dead, in a cave or in a stadium, in a dream or hunting for a frozen burrito at the neighborhood 7-Eleven. Gods and heroes reflect our imperfections, but to paraphrase Prince, we still need them to get through this thing called life.

Yet as a force in popular culture today, with the baby boomers aging into their musical sunset as the light of the rock and roll genre dims, and with demands for cultural diversity growing constantly, our creative and cultural lives are more stratified by demographics, genres, and media platforms than ever. Elvis no longer is everywhere as once he was. Stars, like gods, can fade. But Dylan still is everywhere, a spiritual father of pop purpose whichever way one turns.

This has been the case for almost as long as Bob Dylan—born Robert Allen Zimmerman in Duluth, Minnesota, on May 24, 1941—has been Bob Dylan, a name he seems to have adopted late in 1959. Always musically inclined, first as a rocker inspired by the likes of Little Richard, Buddy Holly, and Elvis (and a heavy dose of whatever else was on the radio in his youth, including Frank Sinatra and other crooners we'll hear from later), Dylan embraced folk in the years prior to his arrival in New York City in 1961, settled into public performances centered in Greenwich Village that same year, and released his first album, of mostly traditional tunes, in March 1962. His breakthrough recording of original material was released one year later. *The Freewheelin' Bob Dylan* contained songs like "Blowin' in the Wind," "A Hard Rain's a-Gonna Fall," and "Masters of War," which permanently changed the template of what popular music would be expected to do.

Once Dylan was *there* as a cultural influence, he was never *not there*.

He's There

Dylan already may have been the most important cultural figure of his era at the midpoint of the 1960s. Music was a hotbed of cultural thriving, and Dylan was at the center of it. The Beatles were already the Beatles. The Stones were the Stones. The Supremes were leading Motown's recalibration of AM radio. There were James Brown's *Live at the Apollo* and Ray Charles's integration of gospel, jazz, country, and rock. Even Bruce Springsteen was already immersed in the first bands he would eventually ride to his breakthrough as one of a long line of "New Dylans." But rock's capacity to carry spiritual wisdom at the scale at which it was needed was not yet manifest. For this music needed Dylan to make his move—which he did.

Over the span of fifteen months, March 1965 to May 1966, he would release three of the greatest rock albums of all time: *Bringing It All Back Home, Highway 61 Revisited*, and *Blonde On Blonde*. "By fusing the Chuck Berry beat of the Rolling Stones and the Beatles with the leftist, folk tradition of the folk revival," rock critic Dave Marsh wrote in 1979, "Dylan...made every type of artistic tradition available to rock."[1]

This was a run that included prolific songwriting and recording, ambitious publishing and film projects, and touring spanning four continents. Shows on the tour included a first set of Dylan's epic acoustic dreamscapes, which had shattered the mold of songwriting for all who followed him by the time he was twenty-three; a scorching second set of confrontational rock with his backing musicians; and walkouts, heckling, and even a famous shout of "Judas!" from formerly fawning fans.

Then it all ended abruptly with a motorcycle crash near Dylan's home in Woodstock, New York, in July 1966. A long convalescence shrouded in mystery followed. It was said that Dylan had died, had sustained permanent brain damage, or had in fact faked the accident to escape his grueling schedule. All but removing himself from the public eye completely for a year, Dylan would not tour again until 1974, once again with the Band, which by that time was acclaimed as rock royalty in its own right. According to the tour's promoter, Bill Graham, there were more than ten million mail-order ticket requests for forty-two concerts in twenty-one cities. That's a stamp on an envelope from approximately 4 percent of the U.S. population at the time.

Today, more than forty years after his *first* comeback tour, Dylan is the most revered artist of his era. His career goes on and on, lauded, admired, and unrepeatable. Pre-COVID-19, Dylan still played an average of ninety performances annually. Known as "the Never Ending Tour"—a title Dylan dislikes even though he seems to have invented it—this string of appearances began in 1988. *Modern Times* (2006) was the number one record in the U.S. when he was sixty-five, making Bob Dylan the oldest artist in the history of the *Billboard* charts to attain top ranking while still alive. (Louis Armstrong came closest with *"Hello, Dolly!"* at the sprightly age of sixty-two.) When "Murder Most Foul" charted at number one as a single in 2020, it made Dylan, then seventy-nine, the oldest artist ever to attain this ranking once again.

Bob Dylan was presented with the Presidential Medal of Freedom by President Barack Obama in 2012 and named a commander of the Ordre des Arts et des Lettres (1990) and an officer of the Légion d'Honneur (2013) in France. He has won multiple Grammy awards, an Oscar, a Golden Globe, a Pulitzer, and the Nobel Prize for Literature. He has accepted honorary doctorates from the University of St. Andrews in Scotland and Princeton University (while being offered and refusing scores more), was fêted by the Kennedy Center in 1997, and enjoyed nineteen weeks on the *New York Times* bestseller list with his amorphous 2004 memoir *Chronicles: Volume One*, all the while selling upwards of one hundred million records. The world of entertainment, fractured as it may have become, was abuzz as one in December 2020 when news surfaced that Dylan had sold his future songwriting royalties for an estimated $300 million.

Rolling Stone ranks his composition—wait for it—"Like a Rolling Stone" as the greatest rock song of all time and Dylan as the seventh-greatest singer. "He changed popular singing," said Bono as part of a panel that made the picks, "and we have been living in a world shaped by Dylan's singing ever since."

He was also the prototype for the singer-songwriter, a new entity in popular music, the artist who not only performed in a signature vocal style, but also wrote all their material rather than singing someone else's.

In praising Dylan, Bono retells a story of Sam Cooke, who wrote the masterpiece "A Change Is Gonna Come" after being inspired by "Blowin' in the Wind." When Cooke played a Dylan recording for Bobby Womack, one of the finest singers of his era, Womack said he didn't understand what Cooke—a revered performer who leaped from the pinnacle of gospel to the heights of pop—meant by sharing with him this strange voice droning these long songs so different from anything else being released at the time. Cooke explained that from that moment on, it was not going to be about how pretty the voice was, it was "going to be about believing that the voice is telling the truth."[2]

He's Not There

In trying to make sense of how his spiritual and cultural impact took shape and what it means, let's turn to a singular moment of Dylan's being *there* and *not there* cobbled together from the stuff of imagination, reality, perception, and myth—a moment that crystallizes what Dylan's influence and relevance have always been about.

Dylan and his posse take their places in a dreamlike reflection on the silver screen in the pivotal scene of Todd Haynes's 2007 film about Bob Dylan, *I'm Not There*. The theme of this scene, Hayne's film as a whole, and much of this book is the same: salvation.

It is the early spring of 1965 in England. Transitioning from an irreverent acoustic hero into a surly rock-star prophet, most of Dylan's official accolades were still ahead of him, even as the music world had already come to look to him as a leader of where music and culture needed to go.

As reimagined in *I'm Not There*, Dylan—played by six different actors, brilliantly so in this scene by Cate Blanchett—passes the time on a long ride with two sidekicks and a nemesis in the quiet hum inside of a classy black car. Bruce Greenwood plays a well-dressed journalist with the patrician accent, stern jaw, and diamond-cutting stare of a very serious man.

Evidenced by D. A. Pennebaker's *Bob Dylan: Dont Look Back*, the documentary film about Bob Dylan that this portion of Haynes's cinematic fantasy draws upon, Dylan was frenetic and funny as he conjured both the destination and the map for a new age of music celebrity, the rock star as a seeker of truth and hipster scene-maker at the same time. This new paradigm for the possibilities of pop both confounded and excited the press, and Dylan amped up its need to understand him masterfully.

The reporter's repartee with the singer in the car in *I'm Not There* recalls buttoned-down journalists sparring with a scruffy-haired, chain-smoking Dylan, whose press conferences had become spoken-word happenings. Questions and answers often went something like this exchange in San Francisco in 1965:

Reporter: How many people who major in the same musical vineyard in which you toil, how many are protest singers? That is, people who use their music, and use the songs to protest the, uh, social state in which we live today—the matter of war, the matter of crime, or whatever it might be.
Dylan: Um...how many?
Reporter: Yes. How many?
Dylan: Uh, I think there's about uh, 136.
[People around him giggle. The reporter doesn't laugh.]
Reporter: You say about 136, or you mean exactly 136?
Dylan: Uh, it's either 136 or 142.

While the press hounded him for explanations about where he was really at and what he wanted, Dylan played with them like a cat plays with a mouse, cigarette smoke curling to the ceiling and photo bulbs flashing.

"You look and sound very ill," Greenwood's journalist in *I'm Not There* says to Blanchett's Dylan, who convulses with a bad cough, raising the back of his hand to cover his mouth. "Is this your normal state?"

Just then, behold poet-provocateur Allen Ginsberg and his driver pull up beside Dylan's window in a loudly puttering golf cart. Dylan rolls down his window to see if it's really him, Ginsberg, one of Dylan's literary and cultural heroes at the time, whom, in this cinematic scene at least, Dylan has not yet met.

As we will see in chapter 4, like any master, Bob Dylan has had many teachers. Ginsberg, played in *I'm Not There* by David Cross, was a pop intellectual pioneer whose creative line of American sexuality, showmanship, and spiritualism linked him back to Walt Whitman, another pioneering poet who joins the conversations of this book in chapter 2. It was Ginsberg who once said of Dylan: "There is a very famous saying among Tibetan Buddhists: 'If the student is not better than the teacher, then the teacher is a failure.'" It was also Ginsberg symbolically chanting and maybe even shuckling in something looking like a prayer shawl in the background of a video for "Subterranean Homesick Blues." That is the famous clip where Dylan percussively tosses away placards imprinted with the key words of the song in a style anticipating mashups of image, text, and sound nearly two decades before MTV standardized this trick for all media.

"What now? What's left?" Cross's Ginsberg asks Blanchett's Dylan, repurposing the words of an interview Nat Hentoff conducted with Dylan in *Playboy* in 1966.[3]

Blanchett's Dylan sticks his head out the window of that black car, answering Ginsberg instead of Hentoff, and looks to the sky. A camera from above frames a deadpan expression: "My sal-*VAAAY*-tion?" he says.

Two words rise with the choppy, nasal, Minnesota-not-so-nice syncopation that many have imitated in homage or jest but only Dylan got to invent. It's an answer imbedded in a question divided into four syllables but stretching itself out like the reprise for an entire career.

After Dylan and Ginsberg shake hands goodbye, both vehicles still moving, the tinkling of kitschy *Twilight Zone*-like music begins to carry out the scene. Smiling like a stoned cherub, Ginsberg veers off the road toward a cemetery, saying: "Well, we'll see what we can do."

Like most of Haynes's film, this exchange between Bob Dylan and Allen Ginsberg is a cut-and-paste dialogue assembled from the canon of all things Dylan: lyrics, interviews, reviews, and legends. With more than forty studio albums, an additional eleven live albums covering only a tiny percentage of thousands of concerts, an ever-expanding official "bootleg" series, shelves of books about him and a few by him, mountains of interviews written and recorded, two Broadway shows, bunches of TV shows and films, myriad dance performances, and a stream of nonmusical Dylan artifacts carefully curated by his ever-clever management team—from collections of paintings and sculptures to a recently revealed vault of Dylan's previously private notebooks, stage clothing, and videos purchased by the George Kaiser Family Foundation for the University of Tulsa in 2016 for an estimated $15 to $20 million—any Dylanophile has an embarrassment of riches with which to work. But it's the simple twist Haynes gleaned for this moment of *I'm Not There* that captures the spirit of Dylan's canon, his vision, and his "right place at the right time" impact on the world. It's those two words: "My sal-*VAAAY*-tion."

Mission and Coercion

Bob Dylan had been wrestling publicly with the question of salvation before those reimagined days in England in 1965. Ever since he was a twenty-year-old new arrival to New York City singing "See That My Grave Is Kept Clean," Dylan's musical personae have believably contained multitudes, an eclectic cast of seekers that have accompanied him until today. In Greil Marcus's words, "in a signal way, he was the Folk, and also a prophet. As he sang and wrote he was the slave on the auction block, the whore chained to her bed, a questioning youth, an old man looking back in sorrow and regret."[4] What most of the figures from Dylan's body of work of more than six hundred songs have in common—whether they find it or not—is the search for salvation.

Dylan's "mission and coercion," in the words of Allen Ginsberg, was bringing the pursuit of the ancient, inextinguishable charge of salvation to the jukebox, radio, record collection, concert hall, and, most important, imagination of a world where traditional religion had lost its ability to do so for millions and millions of people.

Engineering his songs for salvation, Dylan has affirmed the possibilities of the spiritual reach of popular culture, not just popular music. He is musician with interests and skills that carry him creatively beyond his chosen profession. Dylan is also an entertainer influenced by show business in all its forms. He provocatively called himself "just a song-and-dance man" during those mid-1960s press conferences. Indeed, during his early days in Greenwich Village, comics like Woody Allen and Richard Pryor were honing their acts and setting new cultural agendas on the same stages as Dylan and his fellow folk singers. Lenny Bruce, whom Dylan later lauded in song, haunted these stages as well, though his career and personal life had begun to crumble as Dylan became more prominent.

Theater, fine arts, dance, poetry, and all variety of creative expression thrived in the Village too—another reason Dylan was in the right place at the right time as an artist. In the same manner that Dylan describes crossing paths with many of the "traditional" folk and blues artists of the 1920s and '30s "rediscovered" on the folk circuit as his reputation grew, he worked shoulder to shoulder with all variety of artists, entertainers, and "song-and-dance men" immersed in both creative and commercial hustle.

Part of Dylan's act always was (and still is) simply putting on a show. Yet in a pattern of Dylan obfuscating who he was or what his work was about, right around the same time that he joked that his act was mostly showbiz shtick or even a kind of minstrelsy, he also affirmed, as *I'm Not There* assembled it, that his only remaining creative goal was salvation. Tongue firmly planted in cheek, Dylan still made it acceptable and even expected for popular musicians—from Sam Cooke to Taylor Swift—to ask their own versions of the questions of meaning that Dylan highlighted in the vocabulary of pop.

Like Todd Haynes, I hear Dylan's work as a journey through the life-and-death riddle of salvation, his songs like a collection of recipes for redemption, notes and markings in and out of time on the purpose of things, meditations on the possibility of meaning in a world in which traditional myth and ritual have often come to do more to distance people from spiritual emancipation than move them toward it.

Salvation is core to the work of artists with creative vision and stamina deep like Dylan's, and not just in popular music. Culture makers from Franz Kafka to Toni Morrison are the inheritors of those sages and seers from Alexandria to Rome whose questions span millennia. "Bargaining for salvation," as Dylan sings in 1975's "Shelter from the Storm," is what in so many ways brings people to religion in the first place, to a dark night of the soul, to moments of falling on their knees and asking for help, to tears, to love, to hope, to coming home. Great artists in a post-traditional world make great art to address these longings as their spirit and uniqueness move them.

At Dylan's induction into the Rock and Roll Hall of Fame in 1988, a stage to be visited again in chapter 9, Bruce Springsteen agreed: "He [Bob Dylan] had the vision and the talent to expand a pop song until it contained the whole world. He invented a new way a pop singer could sound. He broke through the limitations of what a recording artist could achieve, and he changed the face of rock and roll forever and ever."

Seeking salvation, Dylan affirmed and expanded the possibilities of popular music as an expression of spiritual sustenance and wonder. He also offered a model for living and teaching as a post-traditional person of faith—an iconoclastic, independent, ever-curious, multitudinous person of man and God and law—that had been taking shape for a very long time.

2. Faith

I practice a faith that's been long abandoned

" I do not despise you priests," poet Walt Whitman wrote in "Song of Myself," first published in 1855.

> My faith is the greatest of faiths and the least of faiths
> Enclosing worship ancient and modern and all between ancient and modern,
> Believing I shall come again upon the earth after five thousand years...

A little more than a century later, the late great rock and culture critic Ellen Willis recalled a comment by journalist Jack Newfield in her meditation on the first part of Bob Dylan's career. "If Whitman were alive today," Newfield had said, "he too would be playing an electric guitar."[5]

Dylan himself joined this chorus of influence by repurposing the line "I contain multitudes" from "Song of Myself" to craft the song

17

"I Contain Multitudes," the opening cut on 2020's *Rough and Rowdy Ways*. Name-checking Edgar Allan Poe, Anne Frank, Beethoven, Indiana Jones, and "them British bad boys the Rolling Stones," Dylan claims in his own song of himself that he bridges *at least* four centuries on a good day. That's not quite five thousand years, but it's a start.

Essential elements that make Bob Dylan a pivotal American spiritual figure become clear in the interface between these two poets. Whitman popularizes the lyrical liberation of American free-form verse—later adapted by the Beats and then Dylan—which mirrors the iconoclasm and fluidity of its themes. We might be able to follow this line all the way through to hip-hop. Also like Whitman, Dylan invents and celebrates a self with a singular unique identity that is broadcast to the world as a link in the chain of iconoclastic people of faith over the ages.

Claiming boldly, even arrogantly, the ability to witness all of history in their songs of themselves, Dylan and Whitman are time travelers on a mystic, mythic, salvational American mission. Dylan rarely, if ever, claims to be a holy man, let alone a priest. He usually plays the role of a humble servant beseeching the divine for help. But he still aligns with a new class of believers hailed by Whitman, creators transposing the language and legends of the religious past into a poetic key appropriate for a world getting in tune with contemporary voices of spiritual sustenance and grace.

That a poet would have the audacity to call himself a person of faith while simultaneously rejecting the rules of any traditional religious charter explains a great deal about the world of man and God and law into which Dylan emerged with an electric guitar just as Jack Newfield had predicted he would. Whitman's framing of the mission of the poetic spiritual champions marks cultural shifts from approximately 1500 onward that created the conditions for rock and roll, as well as its musical antecedents and successors, to thrive as a new kind of religious experience, a new kind of faith for seekers of salvation.

A Rock and Roll Empire

The emergent map of Christendom in the 1500s previewed the lines for the future borders of a Rock and Roll Empire. While there is no fixed set of dates demarcating rock and roll's reign, I suggest the approximately forty years spanning from the ascension of Elvis in the mid-1950s until Chuck D's decree about the King and the demise of Nirvana in 1993. Branching out from Europe and including the "New World" of the Americas, the Rock and Roll Empire was a territory broadly defined by the perception of shared cultural roots, reliance on slavery, subjugation and absorption of native cultures in its conquests, and the fracturing of religious communities and identities.

Contemporaneous with the end of Whitman's career and the creative explosion of jazz in the late nineteenth and early twentieth centuries—which happened to coincide with the migration of the Zimmerman ancestors from Eastern Europe to the Middle West of the Golden Land—a range of thinkers were explaining how the role of religion had changed across imperial Christendom.

"We can say," wrote French sociologist Emile Durkheim in 1912, "that nearly all the great social institutions were born in religion."[6] The arts had always been cultivated for entertainment as well as for enlightenment or religiosity, but creative practice, including music, had begun to function as what Leonard Cohen once called "new skin for the old ceremony." Whitman was just one example of a rock and roll ancestor who offered new skin for the old ceremonies of faith using refreshed mythical language for a world in which religion and its priests really did seem to be five thousand years old for fed-up would-be believers—and not in a complimentary way, but as a burden from which to be freed.

David Bowie said that the human race had outgrown its use in "Oh! You Pretty Things" on late 1971's *Hunky Dory*, a song just a few cuts away from his "Song for Bob Dylan." Here Bowie pleaded for Dylan to provide spiritual direction to a generation that he had turned on, tuned in, and then seemingly dropped out upon by the so-called "voice of his generation." Perhaps priests, like humans, had outgrown their use for artists like Bowie, but he, like Walt Whitman, knew that the need for what priests had always done for people remained the same. Passion, purpose, union, tradition, gathering, accessing a higher power—these are the values that the creative arts adapted from religion. They did so without the benefit of religious patrons, who had typically controlled the resources (not to mention the topics) available to artists in Europe, which was the cultural pool where much of the cultural change which would drive rock and roll was beginning to churn.

Modern times meant art for art's sake, and that anyone with talent and a decent platform could express a "Song of Myself" for themselves and whoever else showed up to hear it. Commercial patrons bundled the profits from prophets both false and true through industries for producing and distributing spiritually fulfilling entertainment now untethered from the authorities or ideologies that had previously dominated cultural choices and resources. Corporations, investors, and fans grew an ultimately gargantuan economy of the arts, of which rock and roll would carry a large portion.

Music and other forms of creative expression thriving as "new skin for the old ceremony"—with a religious sensibility but no fixed religious allegiance—were a long time coming. Christendom's equivalent to Bruce Springsteen's hearing the first drum shot of Dylan's "Like a Rolling Stone" as "the sound of a foot kicking open the door to your mind" was the Ninety-Five Theses, a pretty good name for a song by a garage band one-hit wonder even if it's still one thesis shy of ? & the Mysterians' "96 Tears." These theses were banged out by the irascible

Martin Luther in 1517. The Protestant Reformation, which he urged forward, was a response to a variety of social pressures ranging from the intellectual freedom propagated by the Renaissance to frustration with the decay and corruption of the Roman Catholic Church.

Upstart national and regional churches flouting Roman Catholic authority fomented not just religious reform but political destabilization across Europe. Centuries of unrest and a realignment of powers followed. The Enlightenment of the 17th and 18th centuries, also known as the Age of Reason, further upended what historian Jonathan Israel has called the "largely shared core of faith, tradition and authority"[7] out of which people were accustomed to shaping their lives.

In its intensive reliance on rationality and science in the pursuit of human potential and universal truth, the Enlightenment produced many of the social foundations of the world as we know it: John Locke and Adam Smith orienting the world toward market economies; the rise of public education and incarceration; fierce struggles about human bondage and human rights over which Dylan would linger for his entire career; political approaches that urged revolutions that would birth modern nation-states, including one called the *United* States; and science surpassing religion as the central engine for advancing human perception, belief, and progress. These shifts took place unevenly over centuries, but it was clear even during the second half of the 16th century following Martin Luther's death (the era of William Shakespeare, the Bob Dylan of his time) that a rupture had occurred in traditional life across the landscape of Christendom.

These United States of Enchantment took shape both as a result of and contemporaneously with all these changes, basing itself on the model values of "life, liberty, and the pursuit of happiness." Landowning, slaveholding white men though they surely were, the founding fathers crafted a template for a nation progressive enough to allow for an arc—as defined prophetically by another Martin Luther, namely

MLK—that might ultimately bend toward justice. This was an empire that would continually wrestle with questions of liberation for all its citizens.

By the time of the Jazz Age—a period named after an art of expression primarily of African-American origins that rock and roll would outflank just as the Black innovations of rap and hip-hop would eventually outflank rock and roll—the vision of the founding fathers had spawned a nation radically more spiritually and culturally diverse than anything they could have imagined. American music leveraged technology to challenge cultural divisions and hierarchies, including those of organized religion, from which traditional spiritual tropes freely flowed into the realm of enlightened and empowered entertainment.

Four decades after his death in 1892—the equivalent of the time span between Dylan's *New Morning* and *Rough and Rowdy Ways*—the door that Whitman's lyrically, mythically liberated American expression of prophecy and transcendence had rapped upon had been kicked wide open for the generation that further expedited the arrival of rock and roll at scale. Louis Armstrong and Bessie Smith advanced new forms of virtuosic musicianship through courageous innovation of melody, rhythm, and narrative; Robert Johnson galvanized guitar modes that would instruct every guitarist with which Bob Dylan would ever play; millions of phonograph records were sold by mail by Sears, Roebuck and Co.; and Elvis—like it or not—was not long from being everywhere, just like rock and roll.

The period of the early 1960s, when Dylan came of age musically, was the result of all these creative, intellectual emancipations and experiments. Many other areas of expression experienced renewals contemporaneously. James Dean and Marlon Brando popularized the Method, embracing acting as the art of revealing the whole self even though Hollywood was subject to the limitations of the Hays Code until the arrival of films like *Midnight Cowboy* in 1969. Ernie Kovacs disrupted the formalism of television presenters in the late fifties and early sixties before dying young. In 1959, Ornette Coleman, whom Dylan has greatly admired, scrambled the rules of jazz expression. That same year, Grove Press, just down the street from the Cafe Wha?, broke obscenity laws by publishing *Lady Chatterley's Lover*. In 1962, the afore-mentioned Lenny Bruce was arrested for speaking the same doubts and obscenities his audience was thinking.

Modern times were moving fast. The patterns of rock and roll within the tapestry of popular music, traced back from Martin Luther and peaking in innovation in the days of Dr. Martin Luther King, Jr., were stretched across expressive spiritual empires always being born, even as old religious ones were dying. The need for emancipation and salvation drove creativity, truly spawning new ways of being a person of faith in the ever-changing dynamics of man and God and law in the spirit of Walt Whitman's poetic manifesto which Dylan would inherit.

My Porous Generation

Philosopher Charles Taylor asks in his telephone-book–sized speculation on contemporary religion, *A Secular Age*, why it was "virtually impossible not to believe in God in, say, 1500 in our Western society, while in 2000 many of us find this not only easy, but even inescapable."[8] A lack of belief in traditional conceptions of the divine challenged traditional religious needs and sensibilities, but at the same time, spiritual mythology exploded in rock and roll.

Jim Morrison claimed the persona of the god Dionysus on his way to becoming the Lizard King. Mick Jagger sympathetically asked to introduce himself as the devil. John Lennon juxtaposed the role of the Beatles with that of Jesus, resulting in pyres of burning records. Bob Marley rose to stardom as a messenger for the rites and prophecies of Rastafarianism. B. B. King was the King of the Blues, and we've already spoken of Elvis the King. Performers have carried the epithet of godfather, like James Brown, or goddess, like Cher, and there have been many princes—from Ozzy Osbourne as the Prince of Darkness to the artist known and formerly known as Prince, the incomparable Prince Nelson. And of course, overrated and lunkheaded as he may be, London graffiti in the mid-sixties proclaimed that "Clapton is God."

In a world where women musicians, as in all trades even today, are often under-recognized and under-resourced, Stevie Nicks, Joan Baez, and Aretha Franklin were the respective queens of rock, folk, and soul. Like Franklin, probably the greatest vocalist of our era and the musical-prodigy daughter of a famous man of the cloth, there is stellar history of Black performers such as Reverend Al Green or even, for a time, Little Richard, for whom a religious platform or title was elemental to their musical identity.

How did we get here? Why did this iconoclastic, seemingly secular, institution eye-poking movement called rock and roll latch on to mythic titles and honorifics that had served sacred texts, myths, and fairy tales for all of Walt Whitman's five thousand years of priests?

These are the complex systems of religious change and stability Emile Durkheim described, in which religion grounds society even as the volume of traditional practices and beliefs dissipates. After generations of sectarian wars and disputed borders in Europe, the bloody establishment of the New World, and scores of dynamic cultural influences, *Billboard* charts eventually came to demarcate the longitude and latitude of points where societies' fascinations, interests, myth, and history collided with new ways of experiencing faith.

This is also a story of convergences that became more and more personal as time marched toward the "Me Generation" of the 1970s, presaged with an angry, nervous stutter in the Who's "My Generation." This is precisely Dylan's generation, the generation of rock and roll living out a destiny inspired by the fractures marked by the Ninety-Five

Theses through an American culture leaning into premises of "life, liberty, and the pursuit of happiness" and "Song of Myself."

But how did we get to talking about *my* generation rather than *our* generation? Charles Taylor says that "we" was the main conception for living at the dawn of the modern age in the sixteenth century. "Human agents [were] embedded in society, society in the cosmos, and the cosmos incorporate[d] the divine."[9] Interaction with spirits in the material world in the "porous" traditional societies of our ancestors may have been as unremarkable to them as the unseen and seemingly invisible power of the internet is for us. Likewise, our ancestors would have found our unseen networks of communication confounding.

When societies' modes of worship, physical borders, and understanding of rationality and science changed, those porous selves became "buffered," focusing more and more on each individual's unique experience in the world, compartmentalizing the self as separate from the units of a traditional "we." One's mind and body were distinguished from the outer world rather than a seamless part of it. This shift from "we" to "me"—and, in broad terms, from magic to rationality—has a name in religious philosophy that also fittingly describes the state of mind of the Who's angry young men famously smashing their equipment to close their shows: disenchantment.

Enchantment

Concepts of enchantment and disenchantment are terms explained by German sociologist Max Weber, a contemporary of Durkheim in the late 19th and early 20th century, who in turn had borrowed the term from the German poet Friedrich Schiller. The enchanted world is defined by a "we" of social imagination and energy animated by faith, superstition, magic, myth, and chains of tradition both written and oral that connect people to communal meaning within the layers of person, society, and the divine. What we now might of think of as holdovers from the Old World—songs and incantations of mystery and spirit, relics of saints, holy sites and visions, fables and folk remedies, curses, totems, prayers, and amulets that call upon powers from beyond the human realm to protect or enhance human life—are the guts and glue of the enchanted world. They also sound like a dramaturge's stage notes for most of Led Zeppelin's catalog.

Already a century before Charles Taylor, and contemporaneous with Whitman, Max Weber had anticipated that disenchantment would become the primary experience of modernity. The covenantal religions of Judaism, Christianity, and Islam, Weber claimed, had always wrestled with enchantment and disenchantment as competing energies within their systems. On one side was charisma, manifesting itself through religious sensibilities that ignite prophecy and magic, the supernatural, and other esoteric arts for influencing the soul. These are the basic tools of the rock star or musical shaman too, of course.

At the opposite side of this scale of religion rests rationality, which motivates societies' need for the lasting structures that regulate charismatic energy. These are churches and orders and the infrastructure of religious law that systematize charisma—or, in rock and roll, Silvertone and Sears, Elvis's Colonel Tom Parker and Dylan's Albert Grossman, and the phalanx of lawyers and booking agents and pencil pushers that make the business world of music go 'round.

In these contexts, rock and roll bolted toward enchantment— toward charisma, magic, and each individual's having the capacity and hunger to experience the world in their own unique way. The question "What have you got?" as delivered by Brando's "Johnny" reflects disenchantment crying out for direction and excitement despite that character's undeniable cool. Elvis's hips busting through the television screen were just one example of a remedy for malaise.

The phenomenon of a young crooner making people completely lose control was not so different from the hysteria Frank Sinatra provoked at his Columbus Day show at the Paramount in 1944, which prompted a teenage riot that the Beatles' manager Brian Epstein would envy. Popular culture was signaling the need for a reboot of societal energies. People were literally crying out and stomping their feet for it.

From Sinatra to Elvis to Dylan, something enchanting was happening here. But there is one more key cultural element that sets the stage for Bob Dylan to bring it all back home in the mid-1960s, an additional factor priming conditions for Dylan's reflection in *I'm Not There* about salvation as his ultimate goal. This is rock's late-bloomer embrace of a very-much-not-one-hit wonder already teased by Walt Whitman. Ladies and gentlemen, please welcome the Romantics.

How Does It Feel?: Take One

An early shaper of television, comedian Steve Allen ridiculed rock lyrics by reciting them in melodramatic declamations for his prime-time audience at home. Absurdist, purist, and astute, Allen knew something was happening even if he was not quite sure what it was as he read out the lyrics to Gene Vincent's "Be-Bop-a-Lula" in a professorial voice in which the verses of Ezra Pound or T. S. Eliot might be intoned.

In the 1950s, television took its place as a great synthesizer of culture for modernity, networks and channels for what might have once been called the mainstream. Anything hinting at counter-narratives of culture or carrying an axe to grind about the status quo had to be very clever and attractive to get there. But thanks to pioneers like Allen, somehow Elvis and Jerry Lee Lewis wound up performing at the cutting edge of popular culture even as their host laughingly cut them down to size while they worked those circuits and reached all those neophyte believers.

When writing about rock and roll, it's wise to keep Steve Allen in mind. If we take this music too seriously and forget that at its core it is hip-shaking, rule-busting enchantment that often couldn't care less about anyone's fancy-pants interpretations, we may miss the point of the music and wind up twiddling our thumbs in disenchantment all over again.

"If a song moves you, that's all that's important," Bob Dylan said in his 2017 Nobel Prize lecture. "I don't have to know what a song means." In other words, Dylan says in not so many words what he asks in even *fewer* words as the defining question of his age in the chorus of "Like a Rolling Stone": "How does it feel?"

Rock is rooted in Max Weber's description of charismatic magic and ecstasy, expressing something beyond whatever rational tools can be used to understand it—just like our most mysterious and enchanted spiritual moments in religion. If your musical ecstasy comes from a drum circle; chanting; a *niggun*, or wordless melody; silent meditation; or humming the melody of "Louie, Louie"—that feeling is what matters. All the rest is commentary.

Yet holding a balance between intellect and feeling is as important for commentators on music as it is for musicians themselves. Too much talk about rock and roll salvation might dull its magic, but what we lose out upon by *not* doing this intellectual work is also worth considering. A disenchanted world produces soullessness, not to mention it's missing out on a lot of mystery and fun. An exclusively enchanted society, mesmerized by the depth and darkness of its own rabbit holes and lacking rational lenses to frame its desires, can wind up in QAnonville. Not addressing these imbalances has real-world implications.

And this is where the Romantics enter the conversation. Leading figures of the literary vineyards in which Whitman toiled understood that the world before the Age of Enlightenment was enchanted by rich traditions of religious meaning. Then new practices and beliefs grounded in science and rationality sought to liberate Christendom from the imbalances of overly dominant religious authority.

Romanticism called for infusing individual feeling and spiritual community back into a world of the Enlightenment that had strayed too far from the heart. Romantics wanted place and priority for feeling, sensuality, and spirit to keep society open and vibrant despite its rational base. If traditional salvation had been tempered by the Enlightenment, Romanticism sought a re-enchantment of myth and meaning that reinstated the salvation theme in new, more diverse, more personal ways.

Robert Pattison's *The Triumph of Vulgarity: Rock Music in the Mirror of Romanticism* illuminates how rock and roll thrives in the Romantic fusion of feeling, me-ness, we-ness, and salvation. "Two hundred years after the [French] Revolution," Pattison writes, "rock, celebrating this energy, is the liturgy of a new religion…Romanticism is a living popular creed, not a superannuated artistic movement," Pattison says. "… This creed, originally the province of an educated minority, is now by mutation the ideological currency of the Western masses."

Mark E. Smith of The Fall puts it more succinctly. "Rock 'n' roll isn't even music, really," he says. "It's a mistreating of instruments to get feeling over."[10]

Pattison, tying up this Romantic tale, concludes that "Poe's *Eureka* and the Velvet Underground are products of a single cultural force."[11] Echoing Jack Newfield and Ellen Willis, and bringing us back home to the cri de coeur with which we began, he says, "Believing in Whitman, the democrat should also glory in the Ramones."[12]

New Prophets Will Arise

Large-scale audiences for music exploring what Max Weber called "roads to salvation" and Bob Dylan called "road maps for the soul" were waiting for societies' creative class (especially musicians) to unleash its voice. "No one knows who will live in this cage in the future," Weber had written, "or whether at the end of this tremendous development entirely new prophets will arise, or there will be a great rebirth of old ideas and ideals."[13]

Without Romanticism and secularization, the Beats and Woody Guthrie (whom I will get to shortly), Little Richard (since joining Little Richard's band was the one ambition Robert Allen Zimmerman noted in his high school yearbook), and countless other streams of thought and clusters of courageous seekers, Dylan's "mission and coercion" to animate popular music with salvation and faith would not have had a context. But once this context had coalesced, one might even say—as Dylan himself has intimated—*somebody* needed to create a "Bob Dylan" to make its texts.

In the end, it was Dylan who concocted Dylan, inventing himself and his self-creation story in a mode familiar to students of religion and myth. He was a Romantic hero like Walt Whitman, seeking both a self and something to say. Most of Dylan's self-creation myth, of course, was made up, a tale of an orphan riding the rails not long after he was out of short pants, He spun out a fantasy life of a hard-luck hobo from the 1930s, not a precocious child of the 1950s who spent a semester at the University of Minnesota before arriving in New York City.

In "My Life in a Stolen Moment," a poem Dylan included in concert program in 1962, he describes himself as that ne'er-do-well rounder. He mentions influences like Woody Guthrie and Big Joe Williams, but also a nameless band of roustabouts whom he met in his days of running away from home—by his fantastical count—six times. He didn't get caught but one time, he says, and that's the time when he became the Bob Dylan we all know.

Heroes are marked from the moment they come into this world as someone outside of the norm. The strange origins of heroes are part of what make myths tick. Moses was cast into the Nile, discovered by Pharaoh's daughter, and raised in Pharaoh's estate. Athena burst forth from her father Zeus's head. Spider-Man and Batman were both orphans.

While Dylan's family may have had its quirks—like every family and every child of every family—it would be hard to say that the Zimmermans were unusual as hard-striving second-generation Americans in a Midwestern town trying to get the best for themselves and their kids. But Dylan told his tale differently. He made up his own song of himself, imagining his own adventure to match the mythic quest he wanted others to believe.

Dylan thrives in dialogue with a distinctly American conceit that a person can become anyone or anything they have the guts and will to dream, and his singing voice actually personifies this iconoclastic, eclectic self-assemblage. At first this voice made little sense on AM radio stations among Perry Como, Pat Boone, and even Elvis. This is one of the reasons why Albert Grossman, with his managerial genius, had safer bets like Peter, Paul and Mary or The Byrds make some of Dylan's most famous songs worldwide hits in their more familiar voices, not his. So too, decades later, would Adele turn "Make You Feel My Love" into a smash Dylan never could have made from his tired-throated version.

As he invented himself and his voice from the traits and tropes that attracted him most, shapeshifting in the spirit of early poetic hero Arthur Rimbaud's oft-quoted phrase "I is another," it was, ironically, Dylan's *made-up self* that became a bellwether for others figuring out how to discover or make up *their true selves*.

Dylan's voice—how he found it, how it sounds, and what it says—embodies a generational story of re-enchantment, a cultural trope that empowered not just countless kids with guitars to carry pretensions of themselves as an artist with a "voice," but also affirmed a centuries-old trend toward individual choices as the center of spiritual experience rather than those of a community. Dylan-making-up-Dylan became a prototype for a widespread realignment of standards about the "man"—again, a person of any gender, of course—in man and God and law.

The mythologist Joseph Campbell said that "dreams are private myths and myths are public dreams." Dylan sang something like a chorus to Campbell's words in "Talkin' World War III Blues": "Let me be in your dream and I'll let you be in mine."

As he creates himself, tests himself, and fakes it until he makes himself, Dylan's public dream of identity encourages more dreamers to dream their own selves. Faith in oneself becomes a kind of religion in the post-traditional world. Making a self becomes its own kind of personal salvation.

In the next three chapters—about love, teachers, and death—Dylan not only models self-invention, but also suggests that part of self-invention and uniqueness requires addressing timeless questions of God and law as part of the journey. His example of a new kind of person of faith, many centuries in the making and documented in his songs, may offer a framework for a new kind of prophet as well.

3. Love

Where God and her were born

When Bob Dylan entered his sixth decade, Bono was asked for fifty reasons why he thought Dylan was great. "He mixes up women with God" was one of them. This trope is familiar, and so is the intent: "If I could only turn back the clock to when God and her were born," Dylan sings on "Shelter from the Storm," from 1975's *Blood on the Tracks*.

Love is omnipresent in Dylan's imagination, and the intelligence proves this fact—at least, the artificial intelligence. As part of the 2015 launch of Watson, a computer system developed by IBM, Dylan was told in a television commercial that spectral AI had metabolized all his songs and come to a conclusion: "Your major themes are that time passes and love fades," Watson said. "That sounds about right," Dylan replied with a smile.

A love-drunk culture is not Dylan's doing, nor is it the work of the Rock and Roll Empire or popular music or even popular culture alone. This is a reality that developed over centuries, just like the musical

33

trends that carry it and the changes in conceptions of faith and salvation discussed in the first two chapters. But a close listen to how Dylan and popular music privilege love as the dominant cultural narrative of our time reveals tunnel vision in the tunnel of love through which, for better and for worse, many of the spiritual progressions of our society travel. Paying attention to the tales of love Dylan spins, and how he intentionally or perhaps inevitably fuses man and God and law with his experience of love, might be just the kind of spiritual wisdom and affirmation the world needs now.

Old-Fashioned Love Songs

Bob Dylan cultivates many kinds of traditions. One branch of his creative family tree blossomed about a millennium ago in the musical, lyrical culture of southern Europe. In the Middle Ages, peaking in the 12th through 14th centuries, nobles delighted to sit in the front row of performances by a singer serenading them with songs revealing the secrets of the heart. That romantic singer was called a troubadour.

"Troubadour" recalls the famous L.A. club by the same name, where Elton John, James Taylor, Carole King, and a who's who of contemporary artists made it the singer-songwriter's royal court of 1970s rock and roll love. The troubadour of the Middle Ages was a pop-music ancestor for the crooner and pop balladeer, and the *canso*, the *descort*, and the *escondig* provide roots for the love songs of a thousand years later.

Dante (and I will mention this Italian poet from the 13th century often because he is such an essential figure in Western epic artistry) described the troubadour's music as being *fictio rethorica musicaque poita*: rhetorical, musical, and poetic fiction.

Now recall those words of an Italian poet (from his mother's side) from the 20th and 21st centuries. It was Bruce Springsteen who said that "Dylan proved that a pop song could contain the whole world." This statement describes "Born to Run" and "I Love Rock 'n' Roll" and "Love the Way You Lie" too. Respectively, these are stories of American escapism, feminism, and domestic chaos, all of them love songs at their core.

Popular song, like the song of the troubadour, is almost always about love in one way or another, but the trick for a certain breed of songwriter—surely all the best ones—is to make love songs speak about whatever else hits the world in the gut through the language of love. Dylan's embrace of the troubadour legacy expanded the capacity of music to live as rhetorical, poetic, and musical fiction covering an eclectic array of topics about the world, particularly faith and salvation.

The troubadours—and there were both men and women troubadours even though the most common figures in our cultural memory are men—sang insults like "Idiot Wind" and longings like "Just Like a Woman," breakup songs like "It Ain't Me, Babe" and praise like "Love Minus Zero/No Limit" and "I've Made Up My Mind to Give Myself to You." They courted like "Lay, Lady, Lay." They sang to a lover, pleading for her to *please* crawl out her window, just like Romeo sang to Juliet, four centuries before Shakespeare and eight centuries before Dire Straits' rock and roll version. They mourned, they complained, they strutted, they charmed.

It's important to say that male troubadours' female love interests were inspired by a womanly ideal common from the New Testament to "Let It Be" to Madonna. You've heard of Mother Mary, of course, and you'll be hearing more from her in the pages and songs to come. Music, in myth and etymology, comes from the term "muse." The sexual, romantic, spiritual energy of the Muses (the divine driver of rhetorical, musical, and poetic fiction) inspires the musical vessel we use to carry our deepest aspirations.

In thinking about the ways that women inspire and animate Dylan's canon, it is important to tread lightly around the entire concept of muses and the amusements they urge. Dylan's is a male gaze, and so is mine.

There are subtle, profound uses of that gaze, and there are times when Dylan's slips into leering, like in his lecherous role in a Victoria's Secret ad built around his song "Love Sick." Is Dylan a misogynist or a worshipper of women? The answer is likely some combination of both these extremes, not an uncommon composition. He models in songs of love, as in most things, a range of possibilities for what to believe and how to live, but Dylan is typically uncomfortable with any binary stance.

The limitations set by binary sexuality are particularly important in our day. Dylan has obviously left many clues for men to follow in the pathways of love. But what has he offered for those with a female gaze or a queer gaze, or a gaze that does not want or need to choose a gender identity in prefabricated form?

Sex and Love Have Nothing to Do with It

Conversations about Dylan and queerness are growing among a new generation of Dylanphiles charting future paths of inquiry. "I truthfully can tell you that male and female are not here to have sex," Dylan is quoted as telling biographer Robert Shelter in 1966 in a recent piece about Dylan and queer emancipation by Charles Kaiser, which offers a compelling read of Dylan both as a queer ally and pioneer.[14] "You know, that's not the purpose." Dylan continued:

I don't believe that that's God's will, that females have been created so that they can be a counterpart of man's urge. There are too many other things that people just won't let themselves be involved in. Sex and love have nothing to do with female and male. It is just whatever two souls happen to be. It could be male or female, and it might not be male or female. It might be female and female or it might be male and male. You can try to pretend that it doesn't happen, and you can make fun of it and be snide, but that's not really the rightful thing. I know, I know.

Wrestling with gender, God, and law—just as with all spiritual themes—Dylan's thinking tends toward the radical, and his intuitive spiritual wisdom often aligns him with the leading emancipation efforts of his time. He has lived through many cycles of sexual sublimation and expression—demonization of sex in the fifties, the free-love movement in the sixties, the swingers of the seventies, AIDS in the eighties, and today's ongoing obsessions with sexuality, a woman's right to choose, and now the status of transgender people that, at times, seems crueler and more extreme than ever.

But once the desire for recognizing the breadth of the human sexual spectrum emerged as a wedge issue in our era, and the more traditional religions tried to box in gender and sexuality, the more those alternative ways of loving have fought to get out.

The troubadours many centuries earlier faced their own tensions, singing of love in a culture that sparked the triumphalist violence and intolerance of the Crusades. They were required to play on the fringes of the dominant themes of religion to find something malleable enough to hold their feelings about intimacy, while navigating much more conservative worldviews. Troubadors lived outside the law by being honest about love, which assured them a place in society. To recall our very first theme, they played their part in affirming that a person's spiritual core depended on finding an element of salvation through human romantic longing and connection.

Even one thousand years ago, this was far from a new concept in faith traditions. King Solomon's Song of Songs was voluptuously enveloped in love, and later read as an allegory for a transcendent divine-human bond. It was Helen's beauty that left Paris obsessed and burning, and then launched the thousand ships of the Trojan War as part of a full-scale mythic armada. Maybe our dependence on romantic love today has more bells and whistles than that of the troubadours of a millennium ago or the poets who loved the way they lyred a millennium prior to that, but the urge for connection expressed in these great works is the same as that in a garden-variety rom-com. As it says in the title of the song Dylan wrote and his patron and paramour Joan Baez performed, perhaps "Love Is Just a Four-Letter Word." Or maybe, once you really spell it out, love may be the very best way for any one word or person to contain multitudes of meanings.

Probing themes of love through the lens of Dylan, I am trying to peek at what's happening behind the curtain of composition and culture. It's the work of a chemist, or better yet, an alchemist, tracking the manner in which all of the ingredients of a love song interact with each other, and how this interaction results in the transformation of the elements themselves into something new.

Love songs rely upon chemistry, just like love. Records of love and loving are also cultural litmus tests in all the ways a relationship can bring out each partner's hidden self. What are the elements in the mixture of substances that affirm connection to a force beyond ourselves? Some might call merging with the divine, while others might call it falling in love. Is the act of falling in love a collapse of ego boundaries, while real love sets in when partners learn how to continue after those boundaries edge back to their original places like a tide edging back from a shared shore? Rock stars have big egos and big vulnerabilities. Their musical laboratories of love, in their extremes, are where societies' codes are tested, refreshed, and altered. In popular music, intimacy is brought to universal scale.

Better Halves

"Love is born into every human being," Plato says in *Symposium*. "It calls back the halves of our original nature together; it tries to make one out of two and heal the wound of human nature. Each of us, then,"

Plato says, "is a 'matching half' of a human whole…and each of us is always seeking the half that matches us."[15]

Emancipation movements are like a flood, a force that disrupts and washes away even what we think is tied down. A tsunami resulting in the broken rhythms of societal disruption has many unintended results. Black liberation; women's liberation; antiwar movements; gay rights; rights for differently abled people; alternative forms of education, governance, criminal rehabilitation, and on and on—these are all baby boomer interests that have become millennial and Generation X-Y-Z birthrights. They are also all about power and permission, just like core elements of sex and love. Which of these urges started a process that led to another? Barreling over the falls toward a particular good smashes through unplanned boundaries; not just the ones initially targeted, but also those that just happen to be in the way.

The Book of Genesis describes Eve as being carved out of Adam's rib, and a midrash, an interpretive rabbinic legend from about 1,800 years ago, modifies this creation myth by claiming that Adam and Eve were actually a hermaphrodite at first, a single being that was actually a cluster of twos—two faces, two sets of genitals, and two bodies joined at the back and forever facing in opposite directions even *after* they were cut in half to go off and find each other again.

This is a riff on an old Greek teaching about the nature of people akin to what Plato mentions, a built-in longing assumed for every person. As the saying "separated at birth" suggests, we are all looking for a part of us that's missing. A wholeness's being broken seems to be a precondition for the launching of the human endeavor. We begin in harmony, only to be split, and in response to this schism we seek reunion. First there is an undifferentiated universe, then comes the Big Bang, and then the winding path to healing begins.

From the mythic or spiritual perspective, we start as Pangaea—all the continents as one—only to be pulled apart, drifting in separateness, and then carry on as an assemblage project realigning the puzzle. Something about our origin stories reflects this ancient memory, and these myths of coupling are hard to shake and may be unshakable. Dylan seems to agree, with a twist of cynicism at least, in "Talkin' World War III Blues":

> Well, I spied a girl and before she could leave
> "Let's go and play Adam and Eve"
> I took her by the hand and my heart it was thumpin'
> When she said, "Hey man, you crazy or sumpin'
> You see what happened last time they started"

Just Like a Woman

Beginning in 1923, Sigmund Freud—the great dissector and anti-sentimentalist of love—corresponded with the French novelist Romain Rolland. Rolland claimed that Freud's writing on the life of the spirit had missed the point of what life is all about. He told Freud that the "oceanic feeling"—that magic feeling, a not-necessarily-stoned but beautiful feeling—is what matters most. This is the highest plain of human spiritual adventure. Writing with appreciation for Rolland's idea about the "oceanic feeling," Freud revealed much about himself and his intellectual path: "I cannot discover this oceanic feeling in myself," he said. "It is not easy to deal scientifically with feelings."[16]

Feelings are the territory of music and muses, not science. The ocean. The feeling. This is the entirety of the destination of Dylan's journey in some ways, isn't it? Sardonic asides about Adam and Eve notwithstanding, these are his questions for every would-be lover—questions of how to "deal" with how love feels and how to make it last.

These are also the same kinds of questions the Romantics raised up to confront the rationality of the Enlightenment. The oceanic feeling of wholeness can melt away the separation assumed in Plato's dialectic or

Genesis's hermaphrodite. It's a boundary shredder, an empathy maker, and maybe the core human flow that allows for clusters of families and communities to thrive. Yes, sometimes we all share Freud's frustration at not knowing how to achieve this feeling of safety and completion, or at how once we do get there, we struggled to hold onto it. Musicians wrestling with the muses enter the rough waters of a vast and timeless ocean of how it feels not just for their own emotional well-being, but also in service to all of us who listen in their songs as testimony for how they (and we) can work it all out.

Dylan's "Just Like a Woman" is a complicated love song. It is also a signature tune in a formidable lineup of mystic, languid, crystalline melodies on 1966's *Blonde on Blonde*, which some would say is the pinnacle achievement of rock and roll spiritual wisdom. Here is the male gaze again. Here is Queen Mary too, and not the famous ship on a stormy sea, though it may as well be. Queen Mary, a friend, is now a broken little girl as her lover, the singer, stands inside rain, looking at maps with the longitude and latitude of love to try to navigate his way through it.

Can you actually stand inside the rain? Aren't you supposed to stand *outside* in the rain? Or to get *inside* to get *out* of the rain? This is not just some April shower. The singer must be on the very inside of the rain itself, a part of it, within that oceanic feeling and with nowhere to go, that magic feeling both melancholic and all-encompassing.

It was rain from the first and our friend was dying of thirst when he came in here. All he wanted was water, a symbol in mythical traditions of mercy and love when rain comes to irrigate the fields or wash away sin, but also of judgment in times of great storms or floods. We take the temperature or check the barometer to measure the balance of a planet or a person. Natural phenomena in myth and religion, especially relating to the forces of water, often indicate a spiritual assumption. "How's the weather?" is never just a question about the weather. "Just Like a

Woman" offers a forecast of spiritual challenge and instability, a soul more than partly cloudy.

Whatever is off kilter or unaligned for Dylan's narrator-lover, inside or outside, the singer seems to have no choice but to take his chances and get all the way up inside the rain even though seeking that oceanic feeling also poses the risk of drowning him. He doesn't want to know if he can ever stop the rain before he enters it. Ain't it clear? Actually, obviously, it's *not* totally clear. He has found the feeling, but that oceanic, rain-soaked sense is part of a longtime curse as well, a four-letter word for love spelled P-A-I-N in here. And he's stuck with this feeling because he just can't quit.

Dylan is one of the most covered songwriters ever. From Adele to Elvis, Rage Against the Machine to Patti LaBelle, Stevie Wonder to Patti Smith, many of our greatest performers have given voice to Bob Dylan's compositions. We already know that Peter, Paul and Mary made "Blowin' in the Wind" a hit. Jimi Hendrix's version of "All Along the Watchtower" has been said to be Dylan's favorite cover. In the realm of "Just Like a Woman," I am a fan of Richie Havens's version (and could listen to him sing anything, including jingles for United Airlines, McDonald's, and Amtrak—which he sang, like it or not, for the inevitable profit required for the Woodstock liberation prophet of "Freedom"). Van Morrison (with Them)—a genius of an artist whose "us versus them" fixations seem to have rotted out his talent recently—has a killer version of "Just Like a Woman" too. But the most sublime rendition of "Just Like a Woman" comes from the great Nina Simone, who shows just how far an old-fashioned love song can travel.

Just Like a Human

Like a gifted commentator on a sacred text, there are myriad ways to reframe a song with a new voice. There may be fifty ways to leave your lover, but there are at least another fifty ways to tell the story of what really happened. These are the ways of freeing up the inner layers of a song, enhancing and expanding what it means and what and who it's for, a kind of lyrical emancipation.

Nina Simone's version of "Just Like a Woman" traces her own oceanic feelings of hunger, need, brokenness, rapture, and sadness embroidered into an idiosyncratic arrangement, virtuoso keyboard work, and rapturous vocals as well as her subtle shifting of a few notable lyrics. She also cracks open the male gaze, replacing it with a gaze just like a woman's while still maintaining oceanic ambivalence about the moral of the story.

An eminently impressive woman takes over the voice of that little girl in Dylan's original. Maybe it is Eve herself seeking a path back to wholeness to release herself from the longtime curse of Plato and the Book of Genesis in which human beings are remnants of a whole seeking their other half. In "Just Like a Woman" as sung by a woman and transformed into a song about an "I" rather than a "she," its not *just like a woman*. It's *just like a human*.

In Simone's shift from one gaze to another, the flexibility of Dylan's lyrics appears not just for this particular song, but as a sign for the nuances layered into his worldview as a whole. A *human* gaze girds Dylan's vision of love despite his roots in the troubadour tradition's version of romantic love, in which, for example, a Frank Sinatra tune about love as a reflection of beauty through a martini glass would fit comfortably.

Sinatra's cultural trope is almost the complete opposite of Nina Simone's lyrical liberation. I may have missed something on Google, but it appears that Sinatra, who covered Lennon and McCartney, Simon and Garfunkel, and quite a few other songwriters after the era of the Great American Songbook, did not cover Dylan, perhaps the greatest songwriter of them all. Dylan's lyrics don't invite dominating renditions. They require virtuosity and honesty, which Sinatra surely had, but also a humility that Sinatra surely had not.

Sinatra was a believer in the power and pain of love for the entirety of his career, and he surely taught a few generations about a secular but deified, culturally enshrined but binary, boxed-in kind of love. Few musical artists can claim an altar of Western pop romance more fervently worshipped than Sinatra's. But his romantic vision takes us only *part* of the way—not nearly all the way—to love.

A gifted commentator on sacred texts himself, Bob Dylan spent the equivalent of five full albums—*Shadows in the Night, Fallen Angels* (keep your eyes open for how *those* angelic blue eyes made it down here to Earth), and *Triplicate*—singing *only* songs of love that Sinatra had made famous. But long before those recordings, Bob Dylan saw Sinatra's side of the story with his own two eyes through the blue eyes of Ol' Blue Eyes himself.

Bob Dylan hung out with Frank Sinatra one evening over at Frank's place. Apparently, Bruce Springsteen was there too. At one point in the evening, Sinatra took Dylan aside. "He was funny," Dylan said, describing the encounter. "We were standing out on his patio at night and he said to me, 'You and me, pal, we got blue eyes, we're from up there,' and he pointed to the stars. 'These other bums are from down here.' I remember thinking that he might be right," Dylan said.

"It does not insist on its own way," says Paul of love in 1 Corinthians. "It is not irritable or resentful; it does not rejoice in wrongdoing, but rejoices in the truth. It bears all things, believes all things, hopes all things, endures all things. Love never ends." In other words, as teachers across seemingly every great tradition teach, love gently, insistently demands that we go all the way. As the blue-eyed son conversing with the muse, the Chairman of the Board is touched by heaven if we believe his distinction between the blue-eyed singers and the bums. Yet could there be a more precise symbol of the muscular, patriarchal, love-drunk (and as I hear it, just plain drunk) post–World War II romantic America of Dylan's coming-of-age years than Frank?

Bob Dylan went all the way out of *his* way to salute Sinatra at his eightieth-birthday party years before Dylan's full-album explorations of Sinatra, which included Dylan's delicate but scratchy version of "All the Way." At that star-studded event, he feted Sinatra with the song "Restless Farewell," which he had released all the way back in 1964. Its sentiment, lyrics, and melody flow directly from the Scottish ballad "The Parting Glass," a classic drinking tune that had entered the Irish tradition and was a beloved part of the repertoire of Dylan's brothers-from-another-mother, the Clancy Brothers. "Restless Farewell" was Sinatra's request. Love and booze, love and theft, and loving from the bottom of a glass, Dylan and a black-tie-clad ensemble poured out an especially tender rendition for Sinatra.

Songs are like glasses, containers for holding and lenses for seeing. Simone and Sinatra mark the range of possible reflections on contemporary musical love and redemption. Dylan provides a societal looking glass large enough to include images of both. In "Just Like a Woman," Nina Simone invites feminism, her powerful vision of social justice, and an avant-garde flair to redirect a classic boy-meets-girl, boy-judges-girl song that could have hailed in part from the blue-eyed land of Sinatra. With all his sentimental reasons, his otherworldly phrasing, and his crooning, a Sinatra treatment just can't fit the layers of Dylan's writing, though Dylan does important and interesting work in his singing of Sinatra, which has influenced Dylan's choices of repertoire, phrasing, and performance style greatly in recent years.

In the world of the Great American Bob Dylan Songbook and its longings for salvation and emancipation, Dylan's enmity for unexamined love and an unexamined life ensure that he welcomes a sui generis performer like Simone to reflect upon the "broken glass" of "Just Like a Woman" as her own. This is a sign on the door to the musical workshop that Dylan leaves open for all kinds of identities and singers to visit.

Give Us All These Things

Broken glass might reflect the truth even better than the Sermon on the Mount. So Dylan sings in "Shelter from the Storm." Sometimes the parting glasses are empty and the vessels of love cannot contain what we want them to hold. These are sad songs, and the stories of those empty or broken vessels—us—are at the core of his spiritual wisdom.

Psychologist Esther Perel is a writer, teacher, and therapist specializing in the idea of couple-hood. She explained in an interview on the TED Radio Hour that seeking wholeness was the very purpose of any religious, communal, or spiritual ecosystem in the "traditional" world that Charles Taylor described in the previous chapter. It was in an unbuffered world where urges toward community and the divine outflanked overthinking individual needs before the changes in self-conception and religious sensibility spawned by the Enlightenment took root.

This does not mean that Plato or the troubadours ignored lust or love, nor that a serf of the Middle Ages could not fall in love or have a strong sense of self and purpose. It does mean that access to living lives of romance or certain forms of self-actualization or self-improvement were not always accessible or democratic. Even for the most privileged classes, ruling religious and aristocratic systems controlled society, and hence the heights of human feeling and experience one might seek. Fairy tales, myths, folk tales and folk songs, and religious liturgy and lore were where the broadest range of human urges could play out—a field of public-private imagination. Clearly, the fantastical romances and gossip of musicians, actors, and entertainers are today's myth into which lonely lovers cast themselves. The religious pursuit of romance as a driving current of the mainstream is one of the products of modernity, where each of us deigns to live in our own myth of progress toward fulfillment.

Basic social emancipation from the Age of Reason onward slowly changed both the expectations and opportunities for people to seek meaning and joy. But we still carry a lot of baggage from the past—what we are capable of, what our societies are built for, and how and why we feel. And even though in most communities within the sphere of influence of popular music people have the option to seek themselves and their other half in love, it's still a relatively new phenomenon to expect two people to live happily ever in a context where they actually get to choose who they live and love with for themselves. Esther Perel explains:

> So reconciling our need for security and our need for adventure into one relationship, or what we today like to call a passionate marriage, used to be a contradiction in terms. Marriage was an economic institution in which you were given a partnership for life in terms of children and social status and succession and companionship.
>
> But now we want our partner to still give us all these things, but in addition I want you to be my best friend and my trusted confidant and my passionate lover to boot, and we live twice as long. So we come to one person, and we basically are asking them to give us what once an entire village used to provide.
>
> Give me belonging, give me identity, give me continuity, but give me transcendence and mystery and awe all in one. Give me comfort, give me edge. Give me novelty, give me familiarity. Give me predictability, give me surprise.[17]

Love is all, perhaps, but love is not just about love. It's about the purpose of things as well. Counting on *romantic* love alone to deliver us to our port of call with oceanic feeling is a very tall order. Those troubadours were making pop songs that could contain the whole world, but they also were part of a dominant religious system that did its best to harmonize man and God and law.

Surely troubadours worked both inside and outside of these laws, playing both sides of it. Societies always had their "Johnnies"—shamans, witches, holy beggars, hermits, charismatics, and prophets who took the status quo and shook, rattled, and rolled it to keep the central forces of society on their toes. After food and shelter, Abraham Maslow might say, people need love, which means purpose and meaning, which also means something of the divine that's lost in being human in the first place. For much of our history, food and shelter were hard enough. Organized religion or its power parallels took care of the rules of love. These days, thankfully but not without its complications, we want all those cakes and to eat them too.

"My experience was limited and underfed..." the lover sings in "Love Is Just a Four-Letter Word." "Searching for my double, looking for complete evaporation to the core," he continues. "Though I tried and failed at finding any door, I must have thought that there was nothing more absurd than love is just a four-letter word." When we throw love away, as Dylan sings in "I Threw It All Away," or when love and only love *is* denied, that hunger eats our hearts out. This is the place where an equally powerful "Idiot Wind" of disgust can blow, saying, "I can't even touch the books you've read," or "Every time I crawl past your door, I been wishin' I'd been somebody else instead." The anger, the fury of the loss. The emptiness that comes with that loss. These are love letters spelling out a sacred text as well.

Sara

Dylan's personal life is his and his alone. I'm not interested in the least in prying. But in "Sara," a song from 1976's *Desire*, there is a glimpse of an intimate scene on the shore capturing a heartbreaking, beautiful image of the six-letter word—F-A-M-I-L-Y—that love can create, the place where all little boys and girls come from in some manner, and how love giveth and taketh away.

Asked about *Blood on the Tracks*, the so-called divorce album that directly preceded *Desire*, Dylan said: "A lot of people tell me they enjoyed that album. It's hard for me to relate to that—I mean, people enjoying that type of pain." His son Jakob, who lived those years as a child, has described the album as just another side of Mom and Dad fighting. But a lovesick troubadour's audience is drawn to the singer's pain. It helps sometimes to drown inside of someone else's rain.

The object of the urge—the image of the woman Dylan's lover loves and with whom he builds a family, like other ones who pass under his gaze, those who stay and those who leave—who is she? Who are Dylan's muses? In love "Love Minus Zero/No Limit," a formula is offered. It is quite literally a formula: Love, when zero is subtracted, results in no limit. The singer's love, which is a woman, has no limit. She is, in fact, a being who erases all dialectics, all boundaries. We have already heard from sacred texts how opposites in love can melt into a singular whole. Key phrases show how the ideal of a lover balances longing and need by canceling them out:

speaks / silence
Doesn't have to say she's faithful / yet she's true
like ice / like fire
no success like failure / and failure's no success at all

In the final verse of his song, the singer's lover is at his window with a broken wing. She can't fly or escape, and she probably can't come in, because what raven could live in the Chelsea Hotel? This woman is the Madonna, unassailable and perfect, a being holding everything and living beyond measure and category. This is something that our real, contemporary Madonna understands. She created a platinum ideal, embodied an archetype, treated the world with the familiar mythic shape of goddess who called upon centuries of idealizations of women. Madonna then proceeded to scramble that structure with a business titan's absolute control over her image, her product, and the message of her empowerment.

Without Madonna's ironic twist and feminist-capitalist power plays, this ideal—or Taylor Swift's more wholesome version, or Beyoncé, who in my humble opinion puts the entire equation into a new, transcendent realm—this archetype Madonna offered is an impossible identity to hold. Not only that, but the separateness that all the great traditions we have mentioned so far propose a nearly impossible conundrum of human existence: We are separated at birth from ourselves and our others. We seek those others out. And that seeking—well, around 50 percent of the time in the West—leads to the same place that Tammy Wynette and George Jones wound up, with the D-word, that seven-letter word that rhymes with "horse."

Divorce is that broken wing, the one that sent Dylan to nostalgia for Sara at the ocean's edge. Not even the perfect flying bird can carry the weight of a world divided down the middle. We expect too much from love. We seek a god or goddess who can replace an entire village of needs, and a relationship that can flow as full as the ocean but not drown us in disappointment when it turns out to be only human just like us.

Love the Lord Thy God

And this is where another kind of love grows, a manifestation of faith and real-world experience in the embrace of man and God and law. Love of the divine can be part of the formula, flawed as it may be, for a kind of lasting love. It's a love of releasing oneself to unity without dialectic, without division—and perhaps without even a body for loving. From the oceanic feeling to the family on the beach, love and a lover can bring children.

As Dylan's "Lord Protect My Child" makes clear, this is a selfless, soulful love. So too "Forever Young," which gets two renditions on *Planet Waves* (1974) and seems to be based on the traditional Priestly Blessing taught in the Hebrew Bible and still used liturgically today.

Such selflessness requires a third party, or the only party in town for some, which is the divine: Oceanic feeling, playing on the beach, and then a grain of sand infinitesimally at one with all those other grains of sand and no longer alone from being a separate self at all.

This is the same spiritual frequency as "Every Grain of Sand," originally released on the album *Shot of Love* (1981), a peak songwriting moment from Dylan's so-called Christian period that will get a fuller listen in chapter 8:

> I hear the ancient footsteps like the motion of the sea
> Sometimes I turn, there's someone there, other times it's only me
> I am hanging in the balance of the reality of man
> Like every sparrow falling, like every grain of sand

A human being cannot be the beach itself—endless grains of sand—any more than they can be inside the rain. We seek love like the energies of an atom seeking positive or negative charges. It's a scientific fact. And it's exhausting.

Dylan said he was "sick of love" on 1997's *Time Out of Mind* because the love game seems to have no end. But Dylan is not really sick of love, though we are sick of Victoria's not-secret liaisons with that song. He's just tending to his wounds. He doth protest too much. In the end, he makes the choice to be open to pain, which is the reality of the journey. He chooses, like Saint Augustine, another figure who will appear soon as one of Dylan's canonical martyrs, that he will love.

In her 1929 doctoral thesis in German, *Love and Saint Augustine*, which was published in English only in 1996, Hannah Arendt wrote of the conundrums of modernity through the same lens as the martyr Dylan witnessed outside of his window in a dream, longing to be as faithful and full as Augustine in the song "I Dreamed I Saw Saint Augustine" (1967). Arendt—in words similar to those of Dylan—

wrote of the challenge of seeking ultimate completion without connecting with the divine:

> Who will hold [the heart], and fix it so that it may stand still for a little while and catch for a moment the splendor of eternity which stands still forever, and compare this with temporal moments that never stand still, and see that it is incomparable...[18]

Here, love is an act of faith. Again, like the troubadours of old, seeking and declaring one's love is not just a way of life; it is life. It is identity. It is purpose. Finding that wholeness, broken wing at the window and all, is all that there is, a human choice to try on the mantle of the divine, and to love like the divine, but imperfectly.

The impossible miracle of love is as hard to fathom as Adam and Eve's being hacked apart to create two halves seeking each other. If we take these love stories literally, we are likely to believe anything, which is a fundamental fault. The definition of a fundamentalist these days is something like this, one who rejects not only logic but the logic and personhood of others to protect their own narrow understanding of the world. Maybe a fundamentalist in love is one who expects all things to live within a single lover, that the equation of "Love Minus Zero/No Limit" actually adds up to definitive success or failure.

Love, it seems, is about two things: First, it is fundamental, because it's a foundation, a place to be, a shelter, a home for the lonely, divided soul, which experiences its separateness the moment it is born. Second, love is experiencing the possibility of perfection, when God and her were born, as shared in the song with which this chapter began, "Shelter from the Storm."

Dylan has more than dabbled in the ancient texts of many traditions. This idea of the shelter and the storm as the template for love's bloom suits an interpretation, a midrash, not only of his own canon, but also of deep streams of thinking about love and purpose evolving for thousands of years.

God and Her

In Hebrew, a language based on three-letter roots that build a web of words with similar meanings, "shelter" comes from the root for "*mishkan*"—the letters *shin chaph nun*. "*Mishkan*" means "tabernacle," the structure that served as the precursor to the Temple that the ancient Israelites built in the desert. And this word, "*mishkan*," relates to "*schunah*," or "neighborhood, community," the closeness derived from proximity—an echo of Esther Perel's take on that love-fulfilling village. And *this* word, this root, the rootedness of the word for community, relates to the word "*shekhina*."

I am not going to fiddle around with Dylan and Jewish mysticism too much. My goal here is to keep things real by keeping them universal. This is not a Hebrew lesson, nor is it a pitch for the "Jewish element" of Dylan's story. Great works and great artists require all kinds of methodologies to be appreciated. This is one of them, a Jewish trope that can be found in different forms in many different traditions. Dylan has been both curious about and committed to things Jewish over the years, but this has not defined him. It's not clear if it has influenced his work at all. But it does happen to be a mythic, mystic worldview I know well. It also fits "Shelter from the Storm" seemlessly.

So to circle back, this root *shin chaph nun*—"*mishkan*," "*schunah*"—"tabernacle," "neighborhood"—is also the root that gives us "*shekhina*," which the Jewish mystical tradition calls the "female" aspect of the divine. You can call it Mary or Madonna if you like. Some would say it is the Holy Spirit itself. In musical terms, Nina Simone's rendition of "Just Like a Woman" is a *shekhina* reframing of the song. Like Eve, the companion to the first breakup, it provides the missing other (and maybe better) half of the story.

If there are core energies in the world, energies that a seeker seeks just as that energy is seeking the seeker, in our meager human language we call them "male" and "female" as a means of describing difference. The storm is like those elements without the order in the atom—or *Adam*, the first being, who legend says was either a hermaphrodite or provided the rib to make Eve. The storm, that uncontrolled oceanic feeling, that being inside of the rain, is a world without shelter.

Reference to atoms and Adam is fitting because in mystical terms, the godhead is divided, just like we are, into a so-called female aspect, the *shekhina*, which seeks its so-called male aspect to create wholeness again at all times. Spoiler alert again: this is not a binary story. It's a metaphor that attempts to map us all based on a particular linguistic, symbolic tool kit which recognizes that our capacities for understanding and fulfillment are limited as we grasp for truth, something we humans always seem to be doing despite ourselves.

"If only I could turn back the clock to when God and her were born," Dylan sings. If only my *mishkan*, my shelter, my fullest mythical self, could house me with the *shekhina*, the ultimate loving lover. That would be when time itself both stopped and began. But Dylan sings this aphorism as an "If only" phrase. He knows that we can't quite access that clock of love. That's not human time. It belongs to the divine timekeeper. Yet over time, lyric layered upon lyric, and without the hubris of "Love Minus Zero/No Limit" to assume success or failure in hearing what we hear, this is the voice of the moment when God and her *were* born, repeated over and over again. It's also the voice of love. It contains everything even if it is defined by its broken wing. Because just like us, without that brokenness, love could not be at all. Our efforts are on the divine clock doing divine work. Love, then, is a holy mystery, which requires us to invite into our intimacies something greater than ourselves in order for us to feel and be something greater than we are. Here, man teaches God through love, because we cannot live by law alone.

Who Do You Love?

Popular music is about *creating* intimacy with the masses by *sharing* intimacy with the masses. The artist wants to share something deeply personal with the audience, and the audience invites the spirit of the artist into their own private world. Are there any questions more private than "Who do you love?" or "Are you lonesome tonight?" or "Will you still love me tomorrow?" Yet, in the loop of popular music, a singer shares this private unknowing with an audience, and the audience consumes this intimate story both together and alone.

Bob Dylan, of course, has asked a famous litany of questions. The most compelling are riddles for contemplation, setups for responses meditated upon over time. They hang in the air without answers. All of "Blowin' in the Wind" is a set of queries akin to the existential musings of a godstruck psalmist. Dylan's greatest riddle, as I have already mentioned, is definitively answered only by the one who hears it over a lifetime, and comes from what the consensus holds to be his greatest song, "Like a Rolling Stone."

How does it feel? There is no right or wrong answer to this question. It is a charge for reflection and action, even without a clear sense of destination. Being lost by oneself is one thing, but being lost when everyone else is lost too is something else. Longing alone is very hard. Longing in a crowd somehow takes the edge off the hunger. It might even be a place to meet someone else who is hungry too.

Dylan was far from alone in modeling the shift of the grand sweep of religion from a communal concern to an expression of personal feeling. This sensibility places him squarely in the Romantic tradition of poets he has loved, like Rimbaud and Whitman, wrestling with the ancient hermetic teaching "As above, so below." A human is a microcosm of the universe, and modernity has put the individual's desires—spiritual or material or otherwise—above all others. Is God a God of love? And if so, is not human love the divine's most profound gift to creation?

As Oscar Wilde said in *De Profundis*, "The final mystery is oneself. When one has weighed the sun in the balance, and measured the steps of the moon, and mapped out the seven heavens star by star, there still remains oneself. Who can calculate the orbit of his own soul?"[19] For Western culture, and in America as commercially and intensely as anywhere, the solution to this mystery is coupling in love, our ultimate mirror for the self while compensating with the other. In leaving the shelter of divine love, in God leaving the building or that tabernacle being dismantled, new exposures and imbalances appear.

At the Newport Folk Festival, at Forest Hills Stadium, and all across Europe in 1965, Dylan was booed and heckled not just because he "went electric," but because he chose to invest his talents in the mystery of his own salvation rather than in the more tangible mystery of a nation described in the acoustic "protest music" that had made him famous. Dylan called these his "finger-pointing songs." He disrupted a scene clustered around them by pointing at himself, most particularly at his own heart.

Popular music's sun has never set very far from romantic expression, rooted as it is in the troubadour tradition from centuries before. But as the world weaned itself from traditional ritual and dogma enough to make room for these personal spiritual stories to become the core of what we think of today as spirituality, Dylan pried open the gap between individual and collective consciousness so that the rest of the popular music universe could come pouring in. The question is, can personal romantic desire suffice for spiritual fulfillment where grand systems of thought and practice once ruled?

Pulling apart man and God and law reveals gaps, not just in meaning, but in the most basic human need for security, for love. Even an oppressive religious system provides certain protections and benefits. For many, now that the shelter from the storm that religion provided is gone, it is no wonder that the hunger for love and the phenomenon of existential loneliness have increased.

By the time Dylan came to ask the question "How does it feel?" the world really was itching for somebody, anybody, to ask it how it was feeling. And it wasn't feeling so well in many quarters, including those of the heart. People wanted to know why it hurt, and if there was anything that could be done about it. "All you need is love" was surely one answer for the dilemmas of man and God and law, but it's still not clear that romantic love has all the answers that we need.

4. Teacher

Working on a guru, before the sun goes down

———————————————

Tradition is the vessel that holds past, present, and future, compelling time forward but also anchoring it in what came before. It's the source from which we draw the material to shape our experience. "Balance"—that's what Tevye from the film version of *Fiddler on the Roof* called the essence of tradition before launching into one of the most famous songs the world has ever known about the folkways of the Old World. "Tradition," Tevye sings, recalling the Old World after it's almost gone.

In show business and many other rackets, they say that it's who you know that matters. This may be true, but with a caveat. It's what you know, what you carry, and what you teach *because* of who you know that matters. Who you know determines the tradition in which you are formed, and this in turn is how you become who you are meant to be.

The artist, the intellect, the shaman, the philosopher, the priest, the holy man, or the musician are called to introduce communities to tradition and the secrets of man and God and law. For the spiritual seeker, there is always at least one other "who" in the question "Who are you?" upon whom making sense of tradition depends. In Dylan's case, there are quite a few.

That is the focus of this chapter—a fully *not* exhaustive who's who of teachers that led Bob Dylan to spiritual wisdom, and some lessons about what it means to learn and thrive both with the teachers we choose as well as with the ones who choose us. The necessity of putting faith in others animates this set of stories about Bob Dylan accessing his own powerful intuitions and shaping his unique worldview, as he reveals the art internalizing the singular understandings of someone else.

So You Want to Paint?

One of the teachers Dylan has acknowledged most publicly just happens to come from the very same Russian-Jewish-American stock that brought the world Tevye—that idealized landsman crying out for tradition and balance who became a universal symbol for a particular kind of nostalgia for days past.

Norman Raeben was a painter, the son of Sholom Aleichem, the Yiddish writer whose gritty stories about Tevye the Dairyman's scrapping for life and purpose in the old country inspired *Fiddler on the Roof.* Dylan found Raeben running a small art school on the eleventh floor of the building housing Carnegie Hall, the venue where Dylan had performed his first featured New York City concert some thirteen years before.

For an intense two-month period in 1974, Bob Dylan was the rockstar fiddler on the roof, studying painting with a teacher whom he says changed his life. As Dylan tells it, *"Blood on the Tracks"*—which some call his greatest album—"did consciously what I used to do unconsciously…I knew how to do it because of the technique I learned—I actually had a teacher for it."

Dylan continues:

> He says, "You wanna paint?" So I said, "Well, I was thinking about it, you know." He said, "Well, I don't know if you even deserve to be here. Let me see what you can do." So he put this vase in front of me and he says, "You see this vase?" And he put it there for 30 seconds or so and then he took it away and he said, "Draw it." Well, I mean, I started drawing it and I couldn't remember…[anything] about this vase—I'd looked at it but I didn't see it. And he took a look at what I drew and he said, "OK, you can be up here." And he told me 13 paints to get…Well, I hadn't gone up there to paint, I'd just gone up there to see what was going on. I wound up staying there for maybe two months. This guy was amazing…[20]

A result of Raeben's tutelage was the lush musical landscape containing "Shelter from the Storm." Dylan has said that a point of view he incubated with Norman Raeben changed his way of seeing the world so much that his own wife, Sara, could no longer understand him.

Bob Dylan warned audiences in "Subterranean Homesick Blues" not to follow leaders. As such he has redirected the traditions of the songs that first attracted him to music, shapeshifting often as a performer. But Dylan's admiration of and allegiance to his teachers and their traditions, countered by his ability to go his own way far beyond them, has been a key source of the creative tension in his work.

As it is for all of us, what we learn, how we learn, and who we learn with determines much of how we discover the world and our voice within it. We become our "I" (and this very much includes an artist's "eye" for Dylan) based on the "we" of the student-teacher relationship. The teacher guides the student to fit into tradition, even how we become a vessel for it. Then, again like alchemists, students transform both teacher and teachings into something new once they are ready to become who and what they are meant to be. The "man" in man and

God and law is a union of student and teacher enabling each to make and see a new world together.

Learn How to Live

After peeking into the windows of Norman Raeben's art school on the top of Carnegie Hall in 1974, a fuller framing of the curriculum of Bob Dylan and his teachers requires going all the way back to his first Carnegie Hall appearance in 1961, and even a little more.

It is well known that a twenty-year-old Dylan began making pilgrimages to Woody Guthrie just after he arrived in New York City. At first an ardent rock and roller, Dylan developed a taste for a broad range of music, but it was Woody Guthrie who captured Dylan's imagination most as folk music became his primary musical pathway for finding his own voice and place in the world.

"You could listen to Woody Guthrie songs and actually learn how to live," Dylan once said. This is testimony Plato might share about Socrates or the disciples about Jesus. A teacher is a force for molding oneself into oneself through attention and presence, a kind of osmosis, imitation not as the highest form of flattery but as a form of becoming.

It was Guthrie who inspired Dylan to hang a harmonica around his neck and adapt his repertoire, to make up an origin story and change the way he dressed, from the boots on his feet to the hat on his head. Guthrie inspired the affect of Dylan's onstage patter, his offstage persona, his talking blues, his politics, and ultimately—having begun to metabolize Woody Guthrie into "Bob Dylan" along with the many other raw materials he was collecting—Dylan set his sights on meeting him. In "My Life in a Stolen Moment" Dylan may have fantasied how he had pulled up stakes from his family home every year for parts unknown since the time he was but a lad, but it was the desire to meet Guthrie for real that finally sent the eager student away from his home state of Minnesota on the quest of a lifetime in 1961.

Dylan made regular pilgrimages to Woody Guthrie once he arrived in New York City, with his teacher slowly and painfully deteriorating due to Huntington's disease. During visits to the hospital or the house, or at private hootenannies on weekends in the home of one of Guthrie's friends, Dylan would play songs for Woody, a lot of them Guthrie's own songs. The student instinctively wanted to show the master that he had not only taken on the master's traditions but intended to do them better.

Dylan compared Guthrie to the "Grand Canyon" or the "church of your choice" in "Last Thoughts on Woody Guthrie," a poem he read from a stage at the end of a concert at the Town Hall in New York City in 1963. Introducing this seven-minute paean, Bob Dylan said that he had been asked to "write something about Woody…what does Woody Guthrie mean to you in twenty-five words" to be included in a retrospective on the artist. "But I couldn't do it," Dylan continued. "I wrote out five pages and…I have it here…Have it here by accident, actually."

Reflecting upon a character he had once longed to become, and already now a signature character in his own right, Dylan describes reflecting not only for the sheer vastness and possibility of America, but all Dylan wanted to learn from him, which had no limit. And there really is no limit to the desire and hunger for discovery and identity that a student can place upon the teacher—that is, until the hunger for a teacher is satiated and the student determines or is forced to move.

A star student like Dylan laps up all that was the teacher's own, owns it, and leaves that teacher behind. Even in his praise of Woody Guthrie, Dylan hints—surely without malice—at this generational push-pull. He frames his poem as "last thoughts" even though these words are delivered while Guthrie is still alive. In fact, in January 1968, Bob Dylan, who was by then deep into a period of seclusion from public life, joined with the Band to sing at a memorial to Woody Guthrie, who had died in October 1967. Yet Dylan had already given a eulogy for the living five years earlier.

Even if everyone knew Guthrie was dying, it had still taken five years for him to pass. Surely Dylan had come to Town Hall with "Last Thoughts on Woody Guthrie" to praise his teacher, not to bury him, but these were still *last* thoughts, a means of tallying up the creative bill in bidding his teacher goodbye and then taking his persona and artistry with him onward in his journey.

Discipleship—learning from a master or guru to whom willing students give over themselves—is a hallmark of all religious traditions. The New Testament and the Qu'ran are, in a large part, testimonials of disciples. The Maharishi had the Beatles and the Beach Boys. And all those lost hippies had Jim Jones. Loving teachers of profound spiritual wisdom or manipulative fakes, the pattern is the same. Spiritual seekers love to play follow the leader. There are many ways to entwine with a teacher. We will look at a few of them through the lens of Dylan below.

The Gloom of Doubt Vanished Away

Bob Dylan's dream of Saint Augustine comes up more than once in this book. "I Dreamed I Saw St. Augustine," released just after that Guthrie tribute and as mentioned in the previous chapter, is a narrative index of the themes of dreaming, faith, martyrdom, and witnessing found throughout Dylan's canon. One of the key figures in the history of Western thought, Saint Augustine of Hippo (354–430) wrote prodigiously, his surviving works comprising more than one hundred titles. His best-known work, *Confessions*, exemplifies the classical path of suffering a person of faith haltingly travels toward the unification of man and God and law.

As he searched for the light, Augustine presaged a very modern-sounding search for a spiritual home. His proclamations about fully entering faith are akin to the "I Found It!" bumper stickers adorning cars in late-1970s America as the Moral Majority took the American heartland by storm, and the period when Dylan entered the evangelical fold and rapped with similarly smoldering absolutism about the prophecies of the Book of Revelation on stages from Toronto to San Francisco.

Seeking faith can be demanding, disruptive, and extreme. Resolution for the seeker often emerges in a flash of understanding after long periods of stasis or brooding doubt. Augustine's anguish tracked to this pattern, which was particularly prominent among the early Christian holy men and women for whom all variety of spiritual and physical suffering affirmed the authenticity of their embrace of God and law.

"Now when deep reflection had drawn up out of the secret depths of my soul in all my misery and had heaped it up before the sight of my heart," Augustine writes in *Confessions*, "there arose a mighty storm, accompanied by a mighty rain of tears…I flung myself down under a fig tree—how I know not—and gave free course to my tears."[21]

In a scene recalling Isaac Newton's apple to the head or Archimedes's *Eureka!* moment in the bathtub, Augustine's plea for spiritual relief is answered in a burst of assurance delivered directly from scripture, the template for what will define his covenantal faith. After so much searching, he is granted an immutable divine answer to all his questions, vaporizing doubt and initiating him into the life of a believer. In contrast to Dylan's dreamer in "I Dreamed I Saw St. Augustine," who gazes though the windowpane only to find his own gray shadow looking back at him, Augustine sees letters emblazoned with truth that cannot be denied.

"I was saying these things and weeping in the most bitter contrition of my heart," Augustine writes, "when suddenly I heard the voice of a boy or a girl I know not which—coming from the neighboring house, chanting over and over again, 'Pick it up, read it; pick it up, read it.'"

Pick it up Augustine does—the Good Book, that is—and the torrent of his worries is stilled:

Immediately I ceased weeping and began most earnestly to think whether it was usual for children in some kind of game to sing such a song, but I could not remember ever having heard the like. So, damming the torrent of my tears, I got to my feet, for I could not but think that this was a divine command to open the Bible and read the first passage I should light upon...[22]

Just like Dylan describing in his memoir *Chronicles* a shocking encounter with an "apparition" when he heard a Robert Johnson recording for the first time, when Augustine accepts the divine's miraculous invitation to cross over into a new realm of feeling and purpose, he knows that the world that he has known before will never be the same. Randomly opening the text in his hand to a verse from the Letter of Paul to the Romans, he has found the roadmap for the soul that will guide him forevermore:

I wanted to read no further, nor did I need to. For instantly, as the sentence ended, there was infused in my heart something like the light of full certainty and all the gloom of doubt vanished away.[23]

Such redemptive moments of *Eureka!* dot the map of popular music as well. Every major star in the Rock and Roll Empire describes salvational moments of mold-breaking, identity-exploding discoveries of the redemptive power of song from which they will never turn back. Sparks of conversion to the faith of music are core components of rock-and-roll mythology, from Bad Company's "Shooting Star" to Tom Petty's "Into the Great Wide Open." Often delinquents and seekers in their youth, many of rock's shooting stars in the UK—David Bowie, John Lennon, Keith Richards—were dreamy art-school dropouts who fit in nowhere but the oddball world of music and musicians. Once they were turned on to the scene, be it during a fateful encounter mediated by radio or checking out a friend's newest record from America, there was no turning back.

Many musicians speak of Bob Dylan as the central figure of their *Eureka!* Pete Townshend, Joni Mitchell, and Jimi Hendrix reminisced about Dylan's stamp upon their sense of creative possibility. To become guides to seekers themselves, as each of them surely did, these artists first had to open to the wisdom that a teacher could offer to them. Like the tears of Augustine as he comes upon his truth in *Confessions*—or Dylan's narrator in "I Dreamed I Saw St. Augustine" pleading through his tears for something of faith that he can rely upon—spiritual vulnerability is a necessity for binding oneself to a tradition or teacher. This requires naivety and faith. Weeping represents openness to the possibility of transformation. The neophyte roils in pain and discomfort, but then they connect to something huge, and lucidity follows.

Pilgrimage

Popular music has had many classrooms and many curricula. In my rock and roll heyday in the 1980s, this meant a radio or record or cassette tape playing all the time, posters on the wall, buttons clustered like amulets on the front of a jean jacket, and the holy black vestments of short-sleeve tour shirts affirming the dates of a chain of pilgrimages where the townspeople—the suburbspeople, really—gathered for one night and one night only. Though knockoffs might pop up at the neighborhood head shop, those cloth testaments of sold-out (or souled-out) shows from sea to shining sea in particular were also a talisman like holy water or a relic like the fingernail of a saint proving that I had been there, Ticketmaster ticket stub in hand, to witness Van Halen or Pat Benatar or the Kinks.

These were times of blurring boundaries into altered states so that the music and the scene around it could seep in raw. Those pre-show parking lots looked like a temporary village of pilgrims gathered for preparatory ablutions outside of an oracle or temple, everyone chanting the liturgy of favorite songs from encampment to encampment, car stereo to boom box. Hunt, mate, rage, get lost. It all happened at a rock concert, a place of learning many secrets under the not-watchful eyes of the musicians who had brought everyone together.

Once inside for the arena shows or at curtain time for the shells, the amplifiers were turned up to ear-bleed eleven. We pushed as close to the stage as we could get. At a Who concert in Cincinnati in 1979, eleven people were trampled to death trying to get inside the venue. There was always an element of madness at these shows, Crusade-like kids stalking in packs, the screaming and raised fists and smoke, and the vibrations of the music erasing nearly everything *but* the music, even oneself.

And then, after the predetermined encore, emptiness descended as the lights went up. Back to earth again. A few lucky groupies or radio station hangers-on might make it backstage for a bacchanalia with uptight, strung-out, or feckless rock stars, but after a moment lasting two hours or so (four for Springsteen), the master was suddenly gone, traveling to the next date with the next city presciently etched into the black shirt stretched across the backs of thousands left behind.

That shirt would reek of smoke for days, but I would not wash it, maybe for weeks. The tales of adventures, miracles, and disasters from the night before would become gospel in the school hallways the next morning. Like a festival day, a saint's day, a holiday, or a guru's coming to town, we waited for the next opportunity for those gates to open again. The seekers counted the ways they had changed since the alighting, reliving the loop in the grooves of a record turning 'round and 'round until next time, if the band could hold it together and not burn out or fade away.

Sports has its religious urges, a taste of man and God and law in a gathering for the masses driven by its own life-and-death stakes as part of the sanctioned unleashing of some existential craziness for a day or a season. But the rock concert of my youth was where I learned about pilgrimage. The intimacy of danger, loss of control, noise, and losing identity by finding a crowd is part of the popular music pedagogy too.

The Good, the Bad, the Guru

It's interesting that George Harrison, remembered as the rock and roll pilgrim with the richest spiritual CV in the East, played along with Dylan on Dylan's own critique of guru hunting.

"Working on a Guru," an outtake released recently from the 1970 album *Self Portrait*, describes a city in the rain. As in "Just Like a Woman," water is coming down, denoting mercy and openness in the right portions, and a flood of retribution when unbalanced. A singer is on the hunt—sarcastically, it seems—for a guru. He does not find a teacher in this song, and it's not clear he is really looking, but this does not mean that the search has ended. Nor, with a litany of New Dylans tossed like spaghetti to the wall to see what would stick, has Dylan named a single inheritor. However much he may have looked for a guru, he has not wanted to make himself available as one.

Besides his so-called Christian period, Dylan has subscribed to many disciplines. But beyond music, he has claimed no single systemic ideology. There is artfulness in walking between the drops of redemptive rain rather than drowning in total submission to a single tradition. Dylan praises his mentors and teachers effusively, with enthusiasm unmatched for any other topic except perhaps love, but somehow he still keeps his distance from orthodoxies. He also reserves a special wrath, as we will hear shortly, for those posing as teachers who in fact bring ill to the world, while praising on the edge of worship those who bring light.

Dylan's Nobel Prize lecture reveals an abiding spiritual and creative debt to Buddy Holly. This is presumably the only time that formative rocker has enjoyed the company of *All Quiet on the Western Front*, *The Odyssey*, and *Moby-Dick*. These reflections were part of Dylan's speculation about the literary nature of his work in a recorded lecture he delivered to the academy, having skipped the award ceremony.

In Dylan's mythic memory, he and Holly shared a glance just before Holly died. Dylan mentioned this moment of enchantment in musing upon books as soulful companions, the figures of their stories embodied and alive, the lessons taken personally. As Dylan describes all three of his formative reads, he conveys the ways that reading, like music, sweeps him up into something greater than himself so that he can better see and feel the world to its core.

The bookish rock star: this too was an innovation. Dylan has been both an intellectual and an anti-intellectual. He exaggerated an Okie twang in those early Guthrie days, wrote no-caps liner notes like e.e. cummings but with "t" for "to" and all of those "ain'ts" and hemming and hawing. He mumbled and misdirected and adopted Beat slang, jazzisms, and blues and folk tropes. Yet he also hung with the leading poets of his day, sought the blessing (unsuccessfully) of Carl Sandburg, collaborated (unsuccessfully) with Archibald MacLeish, and spoke and sang of Shakespeare and Robert Frost as he read the King James Bible, immersed himself in theater and painting, and was as comfortable in the world of European art films as that of *High Noon*.

The need to renew sources of sustenance for one's faith on the road to salvation means always wanting to learn more. Dylan is an intellectual omnivore, his tastes and metabolism for spiritual substance typically eclectic and unorthodox. Traditional men and women of faith—though there are exceptions to the rule—often hold their passions and curiosity within a strictly proscribed curriculum meditating mostly or even exclusively upon their own tradition. With the notable exception of his most intense period of publicly preached Christianity, Dylan is a Renaissance man of the spirit, uninterested in narrow paths to man, God, and law.

Rock and Roll Library

The period of Dylan's initial search for meaning in the 1960s saw academia opening to new field of study such as American studies, African-American studies, and women's studies, not to mention the first courses on poetry and literature to include contemporary lyrics from popular music, for which the study of Bob Dylan as a poet was a central literary key. Dylan drew a line of intellectual seriousness and reflection across the map of pop. He liked playing the role of a sly, worldly-wise cousin from the country or proto-punk, hyper-hip cousin from the city—and for a Gemini, coming up in patterns of two has its own mystical logic—but he also loved to be a student, to be an autodidact, and particularly to read. Liberating the academy, for better or worse, was another of Dylan's critical impacts.

Jim Morrison, the lead singer of the Doors, who died in 1971 at the age of twenty-seven, liked to speak of philosophy and poetry between the poles of enchantment and disenchantment too. Aldous Huxley's *The Doors of Perception* provided the band with the inspiration for its name. Sophomoric, with the loud voice of a gifted adolescent, the kind of rock and roll kid about whom parents said "there goes the neighborhood" when he moved in down the block, Morrison reemerged as a rock and roll prophet to a new generation of seekers—young enough to be his children, in fact—in those days of buttons on jean jackets and posters and tapestries above beds in the 1980s, mine included.

Part of Morrison's appeal was sexual, his wildness and disregard for authority, his liberal and rampant abuse of alcohol and drugs. But another part of his mythic appeal, juiced dramatically by Jerry Hopkins's biography *No One Here Gets Out Alive*—a genre-launching book that was the first rock star biography to reach number one on the *New*

York Times bestseller list and served as the source text for Oliver Stone's movie *The Doors*—was the intellectual voice Morrison brought from the terrain of rock intellectualism founded by Dylan. He was the model of the sensitive teen with a notebook, scribbling poetry because no one understood. Macho like a jock, but a theater kid too.

To have intellectual passion as well as an anti-intellectual grimace would not be a hallmark for every rock star, but in the pantheon of messianic rockers formed at least in part through Dylan's mold, nurturing opinions about the world based on being well read would matter. As the first rocker to bridge the worlds of the academy and the arena and the bar, Dylan was given an honorary degree from Princeton University in 1970, remembered in a scene part biblical plague, part Keystone Cops in "Day of the Locusts" included on the album *New Morning* that same year.

Going even further back, Dylan was praised for being a top student in high school, even as he was tearing it up at the school talent show. Every high school has a legendary English teacher, a *Dead Poets Society* light in the darkness for teens who opens the door into, say, *Moby-Dick*, *All Quiet on the Western Front*, and *The Odyssey*. Dylan's was Boniface "B. J." Rolfzen. Their intellectual exchange, as well as the possible impact of his encounter with Latin, is covered with expertise and grace by Richard F. Thomas in *Why Bob Dylan Matters*.[24] I will turn to Thomas's enlightening work on Dylan's conceptions of transfiguration as a means of finessing mortality in the next chapter.

Meanwhile, what matters about rock bookishness? Dylan does not want to be presented exclusively as an intellectual. He seems to prefer having a number of identities in his bag of persona tricks at any given time: crooner, blues road warrior, painter, raconteur. In "Murder Most Foul" and on countless other occasions, he reserves his most gracious praise for fellow musicians, but in "Mother of Muses" from the same album, *Rough and Rowdy Ways*, he also praises generals like George Patton and William Tecumseh Sherman for paving the way for the likes of Elvis and, more important, Dr. Martin Luther King, Jr.

Dylan learns from books, from art, from life. This might be a commonplace for anyone serious about educating themselves. But as part of a musical movement that began with busting the chops of authorities of any kind with a shrug of the shoulders, saying "What have you got?"—not unlike Dylan saying "What else can you show me?" after a litany of authoritarian slights in "It's Alright Ma (I'm Only Bleeding)" from 1965— breaking free from the chains of tradition while at the same affirming the concept of the chains of tradition models both the spiritual continuity that has always been a hallmark of generative societies and Dylan's iconoclasm, even about his own iconoclasm. Nothing is sacred, and so is everything. By walking the walk among authorities and academies, leading-edge intellectuals, and street-credible creators as intersecting routes on the same roadmap in the journey of becoming a full person, Dylan models a holistic intellectual liberation serving many masters while serving none.

Spiritual wisdom and intellectual redemption are wherever one finds them, Dylan teaches. They're owned by no one but the brave student willing to seek them out, and this includes a person of any background and at any life stage. Learning, feeling, and growing like this may have started in an eruption of teenage angst, but it became a movement that encompassed all kinds of being alive, seeking justice, and testing both oneself and one's world.

Statues, Stasis, and Static

It's important to note suspect calls Dylan has made when it comes to teachers, those choices which shed light on our own personal and societal tendencies to give up agency when charismatic figures offer simple, ecstatic, or ego-erasing answers to the dilemmas of a seeker's seeking. This is a paradox, that a proponent of such fiercely independent study could be pulled by a spiritual string too. The intensity and extremity of Dylan's late-1970s entry into the evangelical Vineyard Fellowship, for example, with his ferocious onstage raps inspired by harsh, apocalyptic readings of scripture in the tours of that period, are frightening in their surety about a single truth.

Similarly, Dylan's foray into the realm of Chabad-Lubavitch Hasidism at a later stage of middle age—these things happen, you know—also pushes the boundaries of unhealthy allegiance to an extreme. Both the darkening and the enlightening sides of the trust a disciple places in a teacher, exposed to the elements of nature and the soul like a long wanderer in the Grand Canyon without Woody Guthrie by his side, requires a kind of faith in a fundamental, all-in system that transcends what anyone can give, even a parent. After all, people are imperfect and limited until they tune in, turn on, and drop out of their own critical senses to accept all that the system says they must be.

We live in an age of both unrestrained worship of false idols— one of whom even became president—and the necessity of knocking them down. In our day, statues of Confederate figures are pulled down to the ground. Even statues of Abraham Lincoln were toppled in the rage after the murder of George Floyd in spring 2021 in Portland and Boston. Status and statues. Statues and status. When our sense of self becomes so identified with a master, a master plan, or, heaven forbid, a master race, we risk caring so much about tradition that it gets static and freezes, and this blinds us.

Static is the enemy of clear reception. And where did Dylan first learn the difference between good and evil, the good master and the bad? Where did he learn to break through the static of his own childhood, like so very many rock stars and everyday teens of his era? From the radio, breaking through the static from those big stations in Shreveport or Memphis or Detroit that crackled into a childhood bedroom in Minnesota. Dylan was attuned, antennae up, to both learning and rebelling intellectually and spiritually. Radical sounds from the radio in Dylan's generation unleashed pent-up frustration for middle-class American youth, similar to the ways that Facebook, Twitter, and Tik-Tok feed emancipation movements two generations later.

In waiting on a guru, in digging in the most extreme way to a guru's identity, in fundamentalism, there's a kind of madness that can go both ways. One can give up not only oneself but logic, compassion, and understanding, and turn into a maniacal QAnoning shell of a shill or enter a wild hunger to know, to be, to be transformed, to find relief, to escape oneself, to be eaten alive, and then come out the other end empowered. It's a big roll of the dice, a real game of faith, to release oneself to a realm where one spiritual master claims the keys to the kingdom of man and God and law.

Sitting on the Throne

If George Harrison opened a channel to the East, yet another artist often paired with Dylan, Leonard Cohen, shared a similar set of practices and interests. These two had a playful on-and-off connection. Both literary, both poets, both of Jewish birth, at least according to the way a certain legend tells it, Dylan and Cohen had very different creative practices. They also present an interesting contrast in how to live within the boundaries of a spiritual teacher.

"A lot of people have made the comparison between Bob Dylan and Leonard Cohen over the years and there's some hilarious stories," Adam Cohen, Leonard Cohen's son, said in an interview with the BBC's *The Afternoon Show*. He offered his take on a rock and roll tale oft told about Cohen and Dylan. "Like the two of them are sitting in a café in Paris, and Dylan says to him, 'How long did it take you to write "Hallelujah"?'" Cohen's son continued to the punch line.

And my father completely lied to Dylan and said, "Oh, you know, a couple of years"...I think it was [actually] seven years. And then my father returned the favor and said, you know, "How long did it take you to write '[Just] Like a Woman?'" and Dylan said, "Fifteen minutes"...And that's very much about process, I think. Dylan had this quality where he would [shoot] "from the hip," you know, spit and polish, spit and vinegar, and then this old man of mine was much more like chiseling marble.[25]

These are two ways of seeking—the slow-flowing river, resigned to spiritual movement over time, and the fire hose approach of blasting into new places and points of view in an ecstatic moment that purifies and explains everything at once.

Leonard Cohen entered the monastic life in a Zen monastery on beautiful Mount Baldy, about a ninety-minute drive from downtown Los Angeles. There he sat for many years, stoic, seeking, and all shook down in religious routines, carrying the identities of Eliezer haCohen in Hebrew and Jikan, the Silent One, in Japanese.

He followed Joshu Sasaki Roshi, usually referred to by Cohen and others as simply Roshi, his guru, but in the earthiest of ways. In "Roshi at 89," published in Cohen's 2006 collection of poetry and drawings, *Book of Longing,* Cohen recalls his master meditating on the secrets of war, peace, nothingness, and mortality while sitting on the can.[26]

Find the image of a master, a king of spirit, one might say, and he's often posed seated on a royal throne. But Roshi's seat of honor is one that everyone knows like the back of their you-know-what, as he takes care of bodily needs to which everyone is obligated, at the same time as pondering the ultimate questions of the universe. The earthiness of the teacher, the physical nature of a teacher—this is something of the grounding that seems to be essential to the student-teacher relationship. One of the essential challenges of raising a teacher up to model something for which to strive is that when the master gets too high, too ethereal, reality gets lost. Even worse, the guru takes themselves to be of such stature and power, and basic morality breaks down.

Many gurus wind up sleeping with their students. Many gurus are a sham. In fact, as was revealed late in his life, Roshi had abused his standing egregiously and unforgivably with women in his spiritual care. This is a much too common occurrence: the guru and unwitting and even unwilling groupie who is used and used up by the abusive teacher. A teacher must be high, but not too high; on the ground, but not so on the ground as to get lost in the uncontrolled body or the dehumanization of another person's body, especially a trusting and vulnerable student whose faith depends upon the teacher.

Roots

Jim Morrison fantasized about killing his father and sleeping with his mother, hustling Freud into the rock and roll drama of "The End." Rock and roll vowed to die before it got old and not to trust anyone over the age of thirty, and then suddenly Morrison, Jimi Hendrix, Janis Joplin, Otis Redding, and so many more did not even complete their third decades. (In the next chapter, I will be looking in depth at music and mortality.) As it blossomed, rock was a generational acting-out. How would it mature? Could it survive at all? How would it make peace with its roots—creative, familial, and spiritual—while holding to its passions?

The photographer Elliott Landy contributed a photo to the Band's album *Music from Big Pink*. It is entitled *Next of Kin* and was taken on the family farm of bassist Rick Danko, including three generations of the musicians' family members. Dylan ran off and on with the Band for a decade or more. Part of the allure of their time at Woodstock together, during the first portion of Dylan's retreat from the world, was having a life grounded in family and small-town ways. Youth and rebellion have a very short shelf life, and from the beginning, Dylan seems to have demanded casting his lot with both tearing up roots and following them as deeply into the grounding of his creative life as he could dig, telling Mikal Gilmore in 2012:

> Folk music is where it all starts and in many ways ends. If...you don't feel historically tied to it, then what you're doing is not going to be as strong as it could be. Of course, it helps to have been born in a certain era...It helps to be a part of the culture when it was *happening*.

Much earlier, in 1993, he told Dave Marsh that artists even just a tad younger than Dylan "weren't there to see the end of the traditional people. But [Dylan] was." He was referring to artists who had appeared in Harry Smith's collection of recordings from the 1920s and '30s. Some of those artists—Clarence Ashley, Dock Boggs, Son House—actually had a second-round career in the coffeehouses and festivals where Dylan was superimposing his own vision on the folk liturgies they had first recorded. They were on the ground. They were real. And they were sharing stages with Richard Pryor too.

As a second-generation American, Dylan could only trace a somewhat limited line of history in his own family. There was no line to be drawn back to the *Mayflower*, only to Ellis Island. Soon most of what has once been in Eastern Europe was at best a cheap mash-up of nostalgia in *Fiddler on the Roof*. And while there are surely ethnic groups that came to America and preserved folkways and family memories and traditions from the Old World, much of America in the 20th century was about starting over—often with new, Americanized names like Bob Dylan.

Those Americans who had the deepest roots in America—descendants of Native Americans and African-Americans—had had their family lineage and traditions consciously, violently, chronically, tragically, and strategically erased. Looking for roots or expressing them through music and religion may be one of the most powerful elements in shaping American identity because of its plasticity. It's no wonder that so many rootless white kids subsumed themselves in the roots of "traditional people" and "traditional music" that seemed to have the comfort of continuity those children and grandchildren of immigrants did not. One of the great ironies of American popular music is that some its most neglected and scorned populations provided not only the richest trove of creativity for artists of all backgrounds to enjoy, but that the deep, abiding discomfort that formed Black music and musicians (along with, of course, rapture and grit and simple inspiration) provided so much comfort for others.

One Flew Over the Grammy Awards

Popular music is about seeking history and breaking with it, and this is one of the critical lessons Dylan gets and gives as a teacher. Picture the scene. The year is 1991, the year of the Gulf War, and Bob Dylan has been invited to accept a Grammy Lifetime Achievement Award. It is a cultural moment wearing more than a few faces, a moment with the sheen of subtexts both in the moment and looking back on it now many lifetimes later.

Dylan's presenter, Jack Nicholson, himself usually the most famous face in the room, took a lot from James Dean and rock and roll while also surviving to live on and live well. A figure of 1960s liberation from *Easy Rider*, a fighter against the Law who loses both his freedom and his mind after trying to out-hustle the Man in the film version of Merry Prankster Ken Kesey's *One Flew Over the Cuckoo's Nest*, and a prime symbol of the Hollywood godhead where some of the spirit of that liberation landed in a sweet spot combining commerce and art, Nicholson was called upon to bestow a cultural crown on Dylan's head.

Dylan performed a "riot"—Nicholson's word from his introduction—version of "Masters of War" as part of receiving this award for a lifetime of knocking heads in the music business, of which the Gram-mys are known to be among the most market-hungry and conservative elements. Dylan orchestrated a takedown. The song was a song played loud, fast, and CBGB-style unintelligibly on a night of the stars, writ-ten almost thirty years previously at the height of the Cold War. Skip-ping past Vietnam in its time, which Dylan did not much address at all to the consternation of many of his fans, he and his most aggressive pointing-finger song landed during the Gulf War.

Like any corrupt guru stealing life by trying to capture a student in the flesh, the masters of war threaten the chain of life itself, frightening the singer with base corruption and meanness so deeply that he fears becoming a parent himself. That's the kicker line of the song, that those hateful masters break all continuity by stealing the will to make new life.

Already a parent for a very long time in 1991, and at the midpoint of his career—though yes, this was already a *lifetime achievement award* decades ago—Dylan could have been a wise old man standing next to Jack. He could have rested on his laurels, sung a hit or two, raised his glass, and taken up art collecting instead of making art. Instead, with a rakish grin and a nod to his old-time Chaplinesque fidgeting and pulling of faces, he preferred to put forth the face of a mannish boy to match his rolling stone, most particularly that of a blue-eyed son looking for a father.

There is a tradition of the Golden Rule, a distilling of the traditions of the prophets to their crystalline essence: "Do unto others as you would have them do unto you." This is the Golden Rule. So says Hillel the Elder in a slightly different manner. So too Matthew 7:12, and in some form also Buddhism, Islam, Hinduism, Taoism, and Zoroastrian-ism. All have some version of the Golden Rule. Dylan chose a different summary text and a signal lesson from a real but also imagined teacher as he accepted his award for *half* of a lifetime well lived:

Well, my daddy, he didn't leave me much, you know he was a very simple man, but what he did tell me was this, he did say, son, he said...[A long pause and nervous laughter from the crowd as Dylan smiles and either pretends or has actually forgotten what he means to say.] He said so many things...He say, you know it's possible to become so defiled in this world that your own father and mother will abandon you, and if that happens, God will always believe in your ability to mend your ways.

It's not clear that Bob Dylan's parents did much better or worse than most other parents navigating their own second-generation-American sensibilities as a minority group in a small town in the Midwest who happened to have produced one of the cultural geniuses of his generation. Any parent may be limited in what they can teach a child about the way things really are. A blue-eyed son sees too much, perhaps, and tells his ma it's all right, he's only dying, and that his father, the one remembered right in front of Beatty Zimmerman sitting in the front row, didn't know too much and said even less—only that he somehow participates, with Dylan reworking his own myth yet again, in reshaping the Hebrew Bible's Psalm 27, which reads:

Though my father and mother abandon me,
the LORD will take me in.

Football players at the end of a game or politicians on the stump or actors on an award show rostrum are among the many who commonly call out in thanks to the divine when recognized for their achievements. It is a classic American popular culture trope. Dylan offered a social critique of deep resonance with an aw-shucks citation and raised fist (or middle finger) rendition of "Masters of War." This was his prayer and thanks for nothing.

There are the Buddy Hollys and Woody Guthries of the world, masters who shine a light into the darkness to show a seeker the way;

there is the father who does the best that he can with a little help from the divine; and then there is the evil master, the worst teacher of all. What master, what father figure, what owner of culture could be so corrupt, so hateful and hurtful, that Dylan could wish him dead? The master of war. The one he sings about at the Grammy Awards, castigating a master of falsehood while parsing humility and grounding himself in ancient text as he accepts praise for the achievements of (half of) a lifetime, still a son, still learning, still kicking.

North Star

On a walk in a cemetery with Allen Ginsberg in 1975 in Lowell, Massachusetts, as part of the film *Renaldo and Clara* (maybe the same cemetery referenced by Todd Haynes in *I'm Not There*, into which Ginsberg drove his golf cart back in chapter 1) the student who surpassed the teacher speaks about literary heroes and death.

Dylan and the poet have come to praise the buried Jack Kerouac, and they speak of many dead poets, their graves, their names and work, and the traditions they leave behind after they are gone.

What kind of student and what kind of teacher has Bob Dylan become? In some sense, as we and he look back upon all those dead poets, the teachers alluded to at the Grammys that matter most to Dylan, just as they matter most to us. This is the education we receive and do not receive from our parents—where they succeed and where they fail in what they could pass on to their kids. In glue and gaps parents provide, Dylan finds extensions and replacements for mentorship, wisdom, and love. But just as he blurs the line between women and God, he blurs the line between parents, teachers, and the divine. Plumbing the gaps of this conflation, an artist sources models for curricula and classrooms of the spirit, yet another link of self-creation and spiritual recommendation for those seeking links in the chain of tradition Dylan offers for living the meaningful life.

In the Book of Ecclesiastes 12:12, King Solomon writes, "A further word: Against them, my son, be warned! The making of many books is without limit. And much study is a wearying of the flesh." And of books about Bob Dylan, including this one, it can feel like there is no end (in writing it) either. But something about wisdom, seeking it, something about working in and through the work of Bob Dylan, requires repetition and a long haul.

Dylan spoke of Johnny Cash when he died:

In plain terms, Johnny was and is the North Star...you could guide your ship by him—the greatest of the greats then and now. Truly he is what the land and country is all about, the heart and soul of it personified and what it means to be here; and he said it all in plain English. I think we can have recollections of him, but we can't define him any more than we can define a fountain of truth, light and beauty. If we want to know what it means to be mortal, we need look no further than the Man in Black. Blessed with a profound imagination, he used the gift to express all the various lost causes of the human soul. This is a miraculous and humbling thing. Listen to him, and he always brings you to your senses. He rises high above all, and he'll never die or be forgotten, even by persons not born yet—especially those persons—and that is forever.

There's joy in that immersion, that Grand Canyon of knowledge the teacher and their work represent, the North Star they offer.

Some say those who can't do, teach. But that's not right. Rather: Good teachers, they teach. Great teachers, they do. Best teachers, they ensure that *you* do. They draw students to want to sing and write like they do. They initiate the disciple into the inner chambers of man and God and law, showing, but not telling what's behind the curtain. They teach by example with confidence that what they are saying is true. And in being present with a teacher grounded in truth, a student gets grounded in themselves, which is also spiritual grounding and faith—

thanks to the teacher both there and gone—in something greater than themselves too.

5. Death

Death is not the end

———— ▬ ————

R ock and roll has a thing about death. One of its signature scenes is the confluence of a star falling from the sky, flaming out, young and pretty, and going, going, gone. Witness the "27 Club," which has been called popular music's greatest myth. There is, depending on how you count, a cluster of twenty or thirty musicians, from the aforementioned Jim Morrison to Amy Winehouse, who died old in terms of impact but exceedingly young in terms of years upon the Earth, all told exactly seven and twenty.

Why is the loss of a gifted artist tripped up by too-fast living, suicide, or a tragic accident an affirmation of popular music's deepest salvational energies? What makes skirting, tempting, shirking, testing, and sprinting at death such a definitive ingredient in the recipe cooked up for rock and roll?

In the late fifties and early sixties—in songs Bob Dylan must have known well—teenagers kept dying in epic rock and roll car crashes. These were contemporary extensions of the jarring ballads of untimely deaths found behind every hill and dale of folk music. When the dark mark came to teen radio, Jan and Dean haunted the highways and byways of kids with enough of the American Dream under their seat belts to afford a car. It was all good, clean fun with the T-Bird until Daddy took that car away—or until "Dead Man's Curve" took the kid away, even the coolest kid of all suddenly gone.

The draw of death for musicians is as important a part of what makes for musical urgency as sex and drugs and rock and roll. Rock with its burning out and fading away, hip-hop with its recitations of fatal violence and many great stars dying that way, and jazz with some of its most profound figures losing everything to drugs or drink or mental illness. All share a jones for risk and destruction, even annihilation.

Part of the bona fides of the music star is paying a price of serving a muse at its most urgent calling, and emancipating oneself from other possible lives, or dead ends unlived: Kurt Cobain stuck in Aberdeen, Wash., working in a video store unless he played his way out. John Lennon, essentially abandoned, a bad egg, who wanted to be someone other. Jay-Z, a drug dealer, then arguably the second most powerful artist in the pop universe next to his wife, Beyoncé. Chrissie Hynde had witnessed the massacre at Kent State in 1970. With no life left for her back in Ohio, she went to England and invented a new one.

Popular music's acolytes burst out of the pod of their past to escape the spiritual death of disenchantment. Could Bob Dylan have wound up being the manager of his uncles' movie theaters or, as he once said, a teacher of Roman theology if he had not willed his escape? Anything other than being who he was destined to be would have been death. Better to face the affirmation of the unknown than the mortal danger of the expected.

Of course, it doesn't take musical or poetic inclination to know death's sting. Bob Dylan knows just like all of us that everyone has three things in common: birth, taxes, and death. It's also clear to Dylan that we humans are preprogrammed for a paradoxical relationship with humanity's inevitable exit stage right. We fear running out of time, that the knock-knock-knocking on the door and those bells tolling will come too soon. We wonder and worry about mortality, are obligated to witness it particularly unavoidably as we and our peers age. And we are often very good at doing all we can to avoid thinking about it altogether.

One half of life, sometimes the better half but not always, is simply living, thriving, or just plain surviving in pursuit of enough money and food and love and shelter and work and family and health to stay in the world. But the other half of life—much more than half for some—the half that has captured the sound and word of all our greatest spiritual creators, entails wrestling with finding purpose within the finite time one is granted.

"Everything passes, everything changes, do what you think you should do," Dylan sang in the song "To Ramona" in 1964. It sounds like he's singing Plato's song of a philosophical tenet that predates even Plato himself. "Heraclitus, I believe," Plato recalled, "says that all things pass and nothing stays, and comparing existing things to the flow of a river, he says you could not step twice into the same river."[27]

But how much flux can one person take? We know that change is the only constant as we, like Dylan, watch the river flow, and mortality provides a perch for seeing things as they are, the ultimate perspective for a life that won't stop until it stops (though this premise will be tested through the lens of Bob Dylan's spiritual wisdom as well). For many, including Dylan, faith soothes these worries with belief that in some mysterious manner, the equation of man and God and law adds up to the ultimate emancipation of eternal life if one uses one's time in the right way. By facing death, a seeker finds a way to live.

Return to Sender

Not long ago a set of letters came to light, the correspondence between Bob Dylan and his friend from back home in Minnesota,

Tony Glover, a musician and writer. Glover saved those letters, and when he died they came to all of us. We can't help it if we're lucky.

Buried in one of them is the answer to a mystery about the source and intent of Bob Dylan's name itself, about Bob Dylan himself. He was born Robert Allen Zimmerman; how did he become Bob Dylan? How did he *become* someone else, someone new and completely invented? For one thing, Dylan implies in a letter to Glover, when he was coming up, even though popular culture was full of artists of Jewish descent, like performers Allan Stewart Konigsberg (a.k.a. Woody Allen) to Jerome Silberman (a.k.a. Gene Wilder), it was assumed that having a Jewish name like Zimmerman attracted exactly the wrong kind of attention in show business. Zimmerman changed his name so that he could shed an obvious marker of his Jewishness. This real-world awareness is interesting, but why Zimmerman chooses the name Dylan is more interesting.

Even though it has been said that Robert Zimmerman's affinity for Matt Dillon of *Gunsmoke* (and he still often dresses himself and his band like hipped-up *Gunsmoke* outlaws) was the trigger for the name, it was not Dillon with an I-L-L that caught then-Zimmerman's fancy, but rather Dylan with a Y. But W-H-Y?

Dylan Thomas, the Welsh poet, he of raging against the dying of the light, drank and mistreated himself straight out of the light just like a 27 Club rocker. He died at age thirty-nine in 1953 in Saint Vincent's Hospital in Greenwich Village in Manhattan, just eight years before Zimmerman-Dylan made *his* name there—for himself and with a Y— just down the street.

Robert Zimmerman must have seen himself as a poet even if he claims not to have given any serious thought to this particular poet— or to poetry itself, having protested too much about not being a poet here and there in speaking of his own artistry—as he chose this particular name. Even if he selected the name Dylan based purely on instinct or subconscious recollection, the poetic inclination imbedded in his choice is clear. And so too, though he was no one-hit wonder, Thomas's universally famous poem on raging against the dying of the light was surely lodged somewhere in Zimmerman's head as he became the first New Dylan, even if it was no doubt a Thomas.

Whether by activating a subconsciousness memory or pitching himself in a distinct creative direction, Bob Dylan marks himself as a figure embodying society's archetypal dead poet raising all heck with mortality. From the beginning, embodying poets and tracking death have been key elements of Dylan's journey. Music drew him into the same themes as well. The sounds of traditional blues, folk, gospel, and country that urged forth rock and roll overflow with death: murder ballads, good and bad dying young, plagues and wars, and all kinds of bargaining for salvation in the definitively limited passageway of life. Dylan took in all these mortal concerns as he began to shape his art.

Dylan's Nobel lecture along the way and from just plain paying attention that literature—from the classical Greco-Roman writers to the Bible, Dante, Shakespeare, Blake, Whitman, and the occasional Civil War–era poet or Japanese gangster novelist too—have all offered Dylan words soaked in mortality. This is company with which he seems to feel very much at home.

Dante wrote:

When I had journeyed half our life's way,
I found myself within a shadowed forest,
for I had lost the path that does not stray.

Ah, it is hard to speak of what it was
that savage forest, dense and difficult,
which even in recall renews my fear:

so bitter—death is hardly more severe!

But to retell the good discovered there,
I'll also tell the other things I saw.[28]

Much has been said about the "our" in these first words from *Inferno*, the first canto in Dante's three-part *Divine Comedy*. He went down to the crossroads, a plurality imbedded within himself.

This could be a kind of royal "we." Perhaps prior to going down into the circles of the underworld, Dante needs to puff himself up with the assurance of nobility, as if he is someone acting as a plurality, a movement representing more than his single self in order to achieve a level of self-importance or self-protection. Maybe his earthly mind is addressing his soul, which is its own essence visiting from some ethereal place for the fleeting journey of life with Dante as its uncomfortable host. And maybe, like Bob Dylan embodying Dylan Thomas, innocently or not, Dante recognizes that a great poet can never be alone. They carry tradition, other voices, and something that protects the poet against death because poetry is one of those traditions that never dies if it is passed on to the next poet to carry.

The resonance of a poet's never truly being alone on the poetic journey of spiritual wisdom in the face of death will accompany *us* in the pages to come. Like initiations into the words of love or a master teacher, the insistent call to face death requires that the "man"—the *human*—of man and God and law enter deeply into what it means to find spiritual protection and companionship of the eternal kind once they have set out on their own.

Transfixin' to Die

Touching death, realizing how very vincible we are, would have entered the identity of any reasonably aware young person during Dylan's early days as an artist. The country was busily producing assassinations and martyrs as Dylan came of age. There was the lingering presence of World War II, an existential threat in the form of the Cold War with ducking and covering under desks in school and then the Cuban Missile Crisis. There were the masters of the Cold War Dylan scorched in the last chapter, and then the Vietnam War, coalescing mortal fear in the hearts of middle-class white kids that pushed them to take to the streets in protest to protect themselves. Meanwhile a criminally disproportionate number of people of color were shipped off to an unwinnable war and then shipped home in body bags.

If war machines were perhaps a nation's most expensive investment with the very least return, in part to assuage pangs of mortality, American consumer culture trained the sciences on systemizing convenience and safety that denied life's harshness, let alone death. From the mid-fifties, when Dylan's musical and poetic consciousness formed, convenience—and this included advantaging racism, chauvinism, materialism, and jingoism even as demands for emancipation of neglected parties grew—was America's thing.

Penicillin saved everyone with access from once-fatal diseases. Suburbs removed the upwardly mobile from the grit of the city for homes pitched hard for their razzle-dazzle domestic magic, like dishwashers and washing machines and televisions and TV dinners, vacuum cleaners and Mr. Clean, an automated army of new contraptions and chemicals arrived to save, protect, and serve.

Midcentury is when the American Century began, when the frontier (but for the moon and outer space, soon conquered as well) faded, and when it became possible to imagine how one might cheat death. The percentage of people surviving from twenty-one to sixty-four was just over 50 percent in 1940 but shot up to 60 percent in 1960. This was nothing less than cheating death for a certain class of Americans privileged by race and class, yet "quality of life" seems to have pushed Dylan toward speculating about death even more.

Three of the songs on Bob Dylan's 1962 first album, *Bob Dylan*, were traditional reflections about death: "Fixin' to Die," "In My Time of Dyin'," and "See That My Grave Is Kept Clean." Part of this choice of repertoire can be attributed to the social realities shaping the context of Dylan's work, but also the popular theme of death in the music to which Dylan clung, or from reading a book like *All Quiet on the Western Front*, which shook him to the core with its stories of carnage.

Then there's this: Dylan's hometown of Hibbing was just a hunk of iron ore's throw away from the lip of the largest iron ore pit in the world, a gash in the earth visible from outer space that caused the entire city to be picked up and moved to make room for it. The mine also cascaded riches into public coffers that built the grand stage of its ornate auditorium.

Look to the isolation and cold of the Iron Range too, its vast open spaces—not just a massive hole in the ground that would humble anyone, but also the Midwestern laconic way of talking—to find both shadows and light countenancing Dylan's creative character. There are unsaid fears and anxieties in Minnesota Nice. This is the mask of Puritan (or in this case, Lutheran) silence Greil Marcus animates in his riffs on "Clothes Line Saga" from *The Basement Tapes* as an answer song to "Ode to Billie Joe."[29] Death screams at families and neighbors on mute in a small town while everyone around the supper table or in the yard is talking about the weather.

Finally—funny to say, because it is definitely not final by definition—there's another take that explains the *ultimate* give-and-take of Dylan and death that transcends biography, even though biography and chemistry and destiny surely play a role in whatever choice Dylan does or doesn't make about the topics that drive him.

It is a theme highlighted powerfully by Richard Thomas, who teaches Dylan through the lens of his vast knowledge of classical poetry and wrote the highly recommended book *Why Bob Dylan Matters*, mentioned earlier. This is also a theme that Dylan himself—or, rather, his selves—has offered as an explanation for, well, just about everything: transfiguration.

I direct you to Thomas's book for an erudite but accessible explanation and speculation on Dylan and transfiguration. The short version, as explained by Bob Dylan in an interview with Mikal Gilmore in *Rolling Stone* in 2012, is an external answer to the eternal question about Dylan and death and transfiguration. That answer is a member of a biker gang by the name of Bobby Zimmerman who died in a motorcycle crash in 1961 or 1964. Dylan's soul, Dylan suggests, may have merged with that other Zimmerman. This is the nature of the cycle of souls, Dylan explains, and the reason why Julius Caesar, Aristotle, Dante, John F. Kennedy, and Brigitte Bardot will always be around.

Dylan said:

> The thing about it is that there is the old and the new, and you have to connect with them both. The old goes out and new comes in, but there is no sharp borderline. The old is still happening while the new enters the scene, sometimes unnoticed. The new is overlapping at the same time the old is weakening its hold. It goes on and on like that. Forever through the centuries.

He's talking about a transfiguration fixation. It's not the biblical version—not *the* transfiguration—but rather an understanding that time sort of all happens at once. Time is fluid, and its oceanic ebb and flow merges and melds all matter old and new, present and past, like the block universe theory, which describes time itself as an entity that contains all tenses at once simultaneously. This is especially true in identities themselves. All of us could perform endless contact tracing on the people and content that made us—like those teachers in the previous chapter.

A person is a porous container—a porous self, as Charles Taylor has taught in his theories of "a secular age." Recall that Taylor's theory claims that come the Age of Reason, a critical mass of people gradually shifted from essential openness to the guiding influence of spirits, magic, or superstition shielded by rational thought and individualism that filters out the unseen. This includes feeling much less comfortable with the presence of death, and, as mortality decreased, much less exposed to it and reliant on ways of metabolizing what it means.

In raising the idea of transfiguration, Dylan may be yanking Gilmore's and our chains, but he's also making a critical point about the nature of chains of tradition. This is a case for porousness as being elemental to any person's life, including his own, which he claims to believe serves as a vessel for many things beyond a limited sense of self. Not the least of these things is the life force of another Bobby Zimmerman, who died and somehow joined with Bob-née-Zimmerman-cum-Dylan's life force. Such a depiction might sound fantastic, but it's not so removed from the way Dylan merged with the name of Dylan Thomas or the character of Woody Guthrie for a spell when he truly wanted to think, feel, write, sing, or be like them in a hardcore life-and-death-of-a-young-artist kind of way.

This is Rimbaud's famous aphorism revisited (since I have already mentioned it previously) that "I is another." Dylan suggests he is another too—maybe even another Zimmerman. In *another* words, our bodies embody ideas, feelings, experiences, consciousnesses, or even *others* in order that we can be a "we," like Dante or Alfred Prufrock speaking of the self in the plural. In some sense, there is no "I" and no *one*, and not even Dylan-with-a-Y knows why.

A singular identity is fleeting, if it even is at all. But a porous or transfigured identity can go anywhere. Dylan urges forward and models the essential fluidity of time and identity in masks and words. What about an entire generation, the trans community that is proclaiming or reclaiming gender identity without regard to whatever parking meter under which it was born, while the most conservative, reactionary portions of society attempt to legislate these time-traveling, body-and-soul-journeying seekers out of our shared existence?

For Dylan, content to think of himself as previous to himself, and impervious to what others might think about the difference between allusion, reference, or plagiarism, transfiguration means that the sum total of anyone's intellectual parts is not really their own beyond the moment they curate them. An artist is a kind of catcher in the rye for whatever bits and pieces of inspiration fall from the sky, all reenchanted in a moment of creative presence, the way Dylan's art teacher Norman Raeben might paint.

In the way that Dylan's conception of an artist's imagination grants a kind of immortality, his work habits and awareness harken to entering the flow of the river of Heraclitus and Plato, in which nothing is ever experienced the same way twice. Nothing ever dies; it only changes. In this way, Dylan is addressing one of the key obsessions of traditional religions, which invest some of their most concentrated energies into providing comfort and order to believers amidst the troubles of the world. Fantasies of heaven and life after death may have been used as excuses for all variety of bad behavior and control by all manner of religious dictates and authorities, but in bringing a sense of immortality into creative work, artists do not need to wait for death to feel what it's like to live forever—and without the mediation or permission of anyone else.

Free Radicals

Lingering with two texts from vastly different worlds shows how creative work like Dylan's both faces and outflanks death even as it takes it on as a topic. Chronologically these texts are separated by the same span of time as the troubadours and Dylan, essentially the distance between Dante and Dylan as well.

God That Does Wondrously

(El Nora Alila)
God that does wondrously,
Give us pardon,
As the closing hour approaches

Few are Israel's sons, and weak,
You in penitence they seek,
O regard their anguished cry,
As the closing hour approaches

Pouring out their souls to you,
Clear their crimes,
And grant them pardon
As the closing hour approaches

Be their refuge
And save them from curse
Seal them in the book of glory and joy
As the closing hour approaches

Be gracious to them and grant them mercy
And all of their oppressors,
Deal them justice
As the closing hour approaches...

Tryin' to Get to Heaven

The air is getting hotter
There's a rumbling in the skies
I've been wading through the high muddy water
With the heat rising in my eyes

Every day, your memory grows dimmer
It doesn't haunt me like it did before
I've been walking through the middle of nowhere
Trying to get to heaven before they close the door

When I was in Missouri
They would not let me be
I had to leave there in a hurry
I only saw what they let me see
They broke the heart that loved you
Now you can seal up the book and not write anymore
I've been walking that lonesome valley
Trying to get to heaven before they close the door

People on the platforms
Waiting for the trains
I can hear their hearts a-beatin'
Like pendulums swinging on chains
When you think that you've lost everything
You find out you can always lose a little more
I'm just going down the road feeling bad
Trying to get to heaven before they close the door...

The first text is written by Moses ibn Ezra, a Granadan-Jewish poet of the 11th century and an intellectual giant of the golden age of Spain whose influence spanned the Jewish and Muslim cultural milieu at a time when Jews and Muslims were all living in the same philosophical, intellectual flow. His penitential prayer, still sung around the world more than nine hundred years later during Neilah, the final liturgical stage of Yom Kippur, the Day of Atonement, cries out to the divine for one more chance to live in divine grace, with forgiveness, lest the gates of heaven and divine mercy close. Please, Moses ibn Ezra says, let us try to get to heaven before they close the door.

Maybe Dylan knows about ibn Ezra's prayer when composing one of his latter-day classics, and maybe he doesn't. Maybe the thought of atonement and mercy crossed Dylan's mind at some point in his composing or transfiguring of an ancient idea. Or maybe it didn't.

Ideas and longings, if they are truly universal, like mortality, don't need no stinking badges, no passports, no watches, and certainly not a singular vessel in which they must reside. In fact, it's the inability to tie them down that makes certain truths universal. Like a midnight rider or a tune that humanity itself cannot get out of its head, the idea of tryin' to get to heaven before they close the door has no real beginning or end. It plants itself on someone's lips as fleetingly as a kiss, and then off to the airwaves it goes, looking for another. This too is transfiguration; a deep mystery of how living poets find themselves keeping company with dead poets they have never even intended to know. Sometimes poets merge with poets, and they don't even know it.

Death or Glory

It has been said that Bob Dylan was a key ancestor of the punks, especially in the first seven or eight years of his career. This has to do with breaking rules and boundaries as a performer and writer, gleaning a voice that felt distinctly urgent and aligned with many restless souls, and an *attitude* that was just plain punk. How do we know what a punk attitude is? What describes the punk ethos?

It is not the noise or the instruments purposefully out of tune. Yes, the Sex Pistols, real-time legends, made a claim for not knowing how to play their instruments, but Television, Pere Ubu, and Hüsker Dü certainly did. For one thing, punk was community, as coded and generous and competitive at the top as Dylan's folk scene. Whatever other parallels we might find for Dylan and the punks, the core is found in the punk protocol holding that something in the world just isn't right. What attitude is that? A punk attitude is like the Supreme Court's fabled definition of pornography: you know it when you see it.

There is something in the way Dylan manifests rage in raging against the dying of the light that sounds and feels like a precursor to punk, an internal combustion engine of creativity meeting life with a sense not just of wanting more, but of deep dissatisfaction with the vessels into which people are asked to squeeze themselves. A kind of shortsightedness or poor planning between man and God and law limits life force and expression from blossoming to their fullest, and a punk just won't call that a bargain, thank you very much.

Dylan as a punk faces the possibility of his own death—his own martyrdom in an age of American martyrs—in his first record at the age of twenty-one years old. Is this the same urge that saw punks playing out the traditional rock and roll death wish in the violence of pins and razors in their flesh? It's Tupac Shakur and Biggie Smalls playing out ages of rage, risk, and violence to the ultimate edge of hip-hop. It's the Gaslight Anthem's Saturday night special in "The '59 Sound." It's calling out the "masters of war" for death at the age of twenty-three and then again a lifetime achievement award later because they threaten the urge for bringing more life. "Maggie's Farm" is a punk anthem too, its lefty rage about low wages for hard labor and the faceless, elitist "brains behind Pa" breaking the backs of working-class heroes that also suit the Clash's "Guns of Brixton" or "Clampdown" from the late 1970s.

Punk's furious opposition to "selling out," its insistence on keeping music pure of the most crass and musically tempting expression of commerce was also a creed of Dylan's for a long time. The Clash licensed "Should I Stay or Should I Go" to Levi's in 1991. Dylan waited quite a bit longer for deals with Victoria's Secret, Cadillac, Chrysler, IBM, and more, though he did forewarn with an ironic smile at a press conference in 1965 that his music could find itself selling "ladies' garments" someday. Just like legend has him punking the folkies with an electric guitar and leather jacket, he punked whoever still expected the expected in the latter stages of his career by selling the rights to his songwriting licenses for a fortune and pitching his image and music to fill his coffers regularly.

But punk bona fides remain, sellout or no, and "Tombstone Blues," from 1965's *Highway 61 Revisited,* is an even more rip-roaring punk classic. Death or glory, liberty or death. There does not seem to be much of a choice. You either fight for freedom and trust, or you never have a chance to bring anything back home. Maggie's work crew from the previous album *Bringing It All Back Home* is stuck outside in the fields, toiling in the vineyards of song within a power structure that sucks the juice out of the young and hardworking. "Tombstone Blues" brings us from farm to factory table with an anthem about kicking in the teeth of American myth as adamantly as the Clash's "I'm So Bored with the USA" might serve up a kick of a steel-toed boot.

Considering this chapter's speculations about transfiguration, it's interesting that in these blues about a graveyard, "the city fathers, they're trying to endorse the reincarnation of Paul Revere's horse." Maybe this is precisely the difference between so-called plagiarism—flat-out stealing an idea—and the creative lives of the poets, which demand constant embodiment and re-embodiment of content to bring it to new places. When reincarnation is about power, politics, and running people over with a message—that's Paul Revere's horse in "Tombstone Blues"—the intimacy of real community falls flat. It only really works to reincarnate something if you plan to set it free once your work is done.

On the same album in which Highway 61, running cross-ventricle through the very heart of the nation from New Orleans to the Iron Range of Minnesota, is "revisited" as the site of Abraham's ultimate (almost) sacrifice of his son and a precursor to an essential mythos of Judaism, Christianity, and Islam, Dylan recites a roll call of cultural return in

"Tombstone Blues." The ghost of Belle Starr, Jezebel—who is in fact now a nun—and Jack the Ripper (who sits at the head of the chamber of commerce) take turns in a gritty rearrangement of faces and names. Less stately than "Desolation Row," the main song text of the chapter about Dylan and memory to follow (which is also on the same album) "Tombstone Blues" rages and rollicks all night about it all. The singer blasts through the cemetery—or at least the dead space of his mind or neighborhood—while his family is hanging on for dear life: "Mama's in the fac'try, she ain't got no shoes, Daddy's in the alley, he's lookin' for the fuse [though Dylan seems to sing "the food"], I'm in the kitchen with the tombstone blues." They are working for the Man of man and God and law, slaving like Maggie's mom says they must, and there's nowhere to breathe, no light (or nothing to eat), let alone freedom.

Dylan's restless, transfigured raging-against-the-dying-of-the-light poet is tryin' to cook up something in that stuffy, airless kitchen, but even imagining the heavenly dream team of Ma Rainey and Beethoven unwrapping a bedroll won't help when the National Bank sells road-maps for the soul to the old folks' home and the college. Soullessness—the flatness of disenchantment—seems to be the *only* thing everyone has in common. A prearranged, synthetic soul for the young as manu-factured by the bank sounds like death. It offers no spiritual wisdom, no life, whether young or old. And *this* sounds like Dante's purgatory, eternal circles where the half-dead or the should-be-dead or the wish-they-were-dead are stuck in time, static, while Dylan, the traveler, the transfigurer, has to both describe the scene he sees and get the heck out of there, just like in Dante's blues from a thousand years before.

Gratefully Dead

There are the dead lost in the old folks' home and the college, soul-less and mixed up, and then there are those whose presence after they have died only gets stronger, more transformative, more inspiring, even as it forces one to cry real tears. Johnny Cash's eulogy has already been mentioned, but the list of Bob Dylan's departed-not-departed is long: Lenny Bruce, the lost brother from 1981's *Shot of Love*; John Lennon, on 2012's *Tempest*; and just plain walking through streets that are dead in "Ain't Talkin'."

Then there are Emmett Till and Hattie Carroll, real martyrs whose spirits demand singing for justice; or Joey Gallo, the antihero mafioso who echoes a *Godfather-Goodfellas-Sopranos-Irishman* trope as he models nobility and courage despite deathly outlaw ways. There is also "Murder Most Foul," which we are coming to shortly, with its litanies of musicians living and dead adding up in all their musical soulfulness to an elegy for JFK.

These departed all know something that only the dead can know, as Dylan sings in "Silvio," a song he cowrote with Robert Hunter, a key figure in the music of the Grateful Dead. According to "Silvio," when you're dead you find out something you cannot know while living. This idea that only the dead can truly understand and appreciate life, can truly be grateful, or at least inspire grace and graciousness next to godliness, is all over Dylan's canon. Even more important, it's how Dylan shares how he understands his own life through mourning the dead, a ritual repeated often in recent years as Dylan memorializes artists who have passed.

Maybe the most famous eulogy Dylan has ever spoken for a peer, offered as it was long before the now-inevitable march to the back pages of the paper for the generation of classic rockers not felled young, was for the most grateful dead man of them all, Jerry Garcia:

There's no way to measure his greatness as a person or as a player. I don't think eulogizing will do him justice. He was that great—much more than a superb musician with an uncanny ear and dexterity. He is the very spirit personified of whatever is muddy river country at its core and screams up into the spheres...

Personification, Dylan says; a greatness that goes beyond description, that takes something beyond human form. Jerry Garcia is the earth itself. His voice screams up to the spheres like Abel's blood cried out to the divine after Cain slew him in humanity's first murder ballad.

Garcia was for Dylan a colleague whose light defined the friend and co-conspirator viewing him—Bob Dylan—but also nearly defied description. Only death set these feelings free, just as it set free the soulful inheritance that the body held for all who followed.

The most common story of a mythic grateful dead—a phrase the band picked out of lexicon one day when fate guided one of Jerry's remaining fingers to just the right page under the letter "G"—involves a traveler who finds the corpse of a person who never received a proper burial, typically as a result of an unpaid debt. The traveler then either pays off the dead person's debt or pays for the burial. There's a reward for this deed, which comes only later, when the Good Samaritan's life is saved by a person or animal who is actually the transfigured soul of that grateful dead fellow.

It would take more than an extended session of "Space," the Grateful Dead's traditional, seemingly endless instrumental jam, to tell a reasonably informative tale about the band called the Grateful Dead, but the story of Dylan and the Dead as a unit is actually both long and short. It's long in that the Dead gratefully played Dylan tunes throughout their career, with the best Dead family versions of his tunes coming from Jerry Garcia as a solo artist or the Jerry Garcia Band, whose versions of "Tangled Up in Blue," "Simple Twist of Fate," "Going, Going, Gone," and "Señor" give even more soul to some of Dylan's most profound compositions. The short version of Dylan and the Dead was just six concerts. They had rehearsed upwards of eighty songs, both Dylan's and others', then disbanded for forty-five days and forgot most of them, playing those few shows to mixed reviews.

This was by many accounts a Rip van Winkle period in Dylan's career, the 1980s. It was also a time, sun shining in Reagan's America, that the Deadhead business grew wildly, animated by the hit single "Touch of Grey" and MTV in 1987 in ways that surprised the artists and many of its fans—a wave of seekers of enchantment.

It's said in the rabbinic teachings of late antiquity, some 1,800 years ago—which really isn't that far into the past when you think about it in terms of soul and transfiguration—that sleep is one-sixtieth of death. This theme is reflected in stories of the holy sleeper, be it the tale of Jonah, who rises to his purpose to go to Nineveh after a deep sleep on a ship and a symbolic death in the giant fish, only to be disappointed by a too-forgiving divine will; or of Rip van Winkle, who misses out on the American Revolution and realizes he can never get back in tune with the times. Sleep and dreams preview our tenuous grip on life even when we are living.

"Give me liberty or give me death," Patrick Henry said famously in the same year when Rip Van Winkle was imagined by Washington Irving. Liberty and America. Death and emancipation. Proclamations and freedom in the culture and celebrations of song.

The Dead made their name first as soundtrack trippers for an escape from the drudgery of disenchanted existence into the limitlessness of psychedelia. It was music of escape and enchantment, disembodiment and magic—more of Max Weber's sociological theories in the flesh. Revelation. Release. Return. Repeat. The acid test. Borderlessness. Boundlessness. Liberty.

Amazingly, the Dead came back grateful and wildly popular in the 1980s, when the hippies were on Wall Street as much as down on the farm. Yes, theirs was a dark and scary musical vision of America. Jerry Garcia in particular was said to have carried much pain. Why else did he head to heroin from the highs and lows of LSD? The Dead's songs are full of borderline angels, lost ghosts, murder, an underbelly of fears despite the sheer joy in the playing. This is the dichotomy of their name and their essence. Grateful. Gracious. Grace. But these graces are only granted because of death, the ultimate test for the fats, acids, fluids, minerals, and other viscera that house our souls.

Part of Dylan's deep love for Jerry Garcia was surely musical, just as he says, but also due to Jerry's innate ability to enter into the big muddy—to *be* the big muddy—to sing to and with the spheres in a way that, like Silvio, only dead men know. He waded in with his spirit, at least in what we saw and heard of it, as far as the transmigratory pool would allow. The Dead were part Mardi Gras, part All Souls' Day. Part darkness, part light. Part disembodiment, part decay—both this world and the next.

Wake-Up Call

We all know death. We all know that no one gets out of here alive. At the time of this writing, we may know death more intimately than at any time since our great-grandparents or earlier. Dylan met the COVID-19 pandemic with a counterpunch, or perhaps absorption of the blows, through the surprise masterwork of *Rough and Rowdy Ways*, which rhapsodizes love, music, muses, and memory as a comfort to ride out the plague. The troubadours worked as a movement until the Black Death swept through Europe, but the songs survived. Which songs will survive our darkness?

America elected a man as old as Bob Dylan to redirect nature's fury and assuage its exhaustion, replacing the one who had stood with his supporters while the death count got higher, the callousness calcified, and he twirled his fingers to the song "YMCA" at campaign rallies. Imagine using the signature song of a group of gay men who somehow rode out the plague of the AIDS epidemic, the Village People (coming up and out a decade after Dylan's Greenwich Village community), to soundtrack obliviousness during the next great plague by a figure who provided sanction and cover for vile expressions of homophobia without even a wisp of irony.

COVID-19 knows irony, but not mercy. It made a saint out of John Prine, who had obviously smoked a cigarette nine miles long in preparation for the end. But still, John Prine at a time like this? It took Adam Schlesinger from Fountains of Wayne as well as the great popular music retrospectivist Hal Willner, and darkened the doorway of many musicians more. It crushed the touring industry—even the Never Ending Tour—while titans of popular music performed from their living rooms and home studios and filled the air with tweets and IMs and podcasts about the same things all of us were feeling: loneliness, fear of death, the pang of loss, and the loss of control. It did not matter—at least for a little while—who was considered great. Anyone with two feet on the ground could feel it shaking, and everyone was—for a moment—a little bit the same.

The great and grateful artist knows these longings long before any trigger, and Dylan has always been that way. He seeks what is mortal, prods it, visits those places with a Virgil or a Jerry Garcia, and migrates through the boundless, unearthly realm where time, like an ocean, does not define where it begins or ends. An era when just being able to breathe is too often a medical or social luxury reminds us viscerally that true enlightenment often comes only in the contours revealed by the shadows of deepest loss.

We will know very soon, or perhaps we already know, whether COVID-19 will leave behind a residue of humility, something of the sameness that means collective caring and shared fate. Will the graciousness expressed for suddenly "essential" have-not workers managing the infrastructure and distribution lines for the "haves," and for selfless medical professionals abide? Will the grace some found in seeking out purpose at a time of death transfigure into lives of graciousness?

Bob Dylan came forward in a unique and timely way with *Rough and Rowdy Ways* to heighten these questions, expressing a dialogue with mortality when God really did seem to have left the building. Perhaps all the suffering and disruption of the COVID-19 era are an invitation to fill the building and all variety of houses of worship with reenchanted ways of making meaning in the face of mortality, or even to invite the divine back inside our spaces and voices in new ways.

When a president had the audacity to stand outside of a church with an upside-down Bible while peaceful protesters were sprayed with tear gas and a pandemic raged despite denials, it was very easy to want to give up, make like Elvis, and leave the building—and the country and the world too. But the vacancy sign for empathy displayed by the man supposedly holding the highest office of the law of the land, just like death, inadvertently offered an undeniable warning to live better, fight for justice harder, change the guard sooner, and realign the man and God and law continuum with other truths right away. Mortality, as always, was the wake-up call, and the ultimate test of faith.

God

6. Memory

I had to rearrange their faces and give them all another name

---

When Mikal Gilmore of *Rolling Stone* asked Bob Dylan about the significance of the release of his album *Love and Theft* on September 11, 2001, Dylan offered an image reflecting both the destruction and the loss of life on that day as well as the essence of how he works as a songwriter. "I mean, you're talking to a person that feels like he's walking around in the ruins of Pompeii all the time," he said. "It's always been that way for one reason or another."[30]

Pompeii is frozen in time at the far end of the classical world, but the classics of Greece and Rome, which we might think of as static and unchanging, were in fact the result of a lively, dynamic set of creative practices evolving for many centuries. Walking metaphorically through the ruins of Pompeii, Dylan reflects a source of creativity that not only drives his music making, but suggests a conception of an ever-renewed past essential to a life of spiritual wisdom today.

Before entering further into the realms of Dylan and the art of memory, let's note that Chapter 6 marks a shift in focus. We began this book with the premise that, like sages and seekers over thousands of years, Dylan's creative journey is driven by innate hunger for salvation. He is born to a world in which music emerges with its charismatic, spiritual nature and deep roots in ritual, mythic expression to play a leading role in generating answers to ancient salvational questions that fused themselves to contemporary social urges for sexual, civil, and social emancipation.

Through themes of love, teachers, and death, Dylan harvests the dynamic interaction of the layers of meaning planted on Maggie's farm—of what it means to be a person in the holy trinity of man and God and law. Examining these three elements of spiritual wisdom separately and together, powerful spiritual roadmaps for the soul emerge. How we love, learn, and die are the essential acts of our being, of being a person, of being a "man."

Now it's time to look more closely at the landscapes in which Dylan places these human stories. This requires the second of those three words: God. We are talking about a theological blues in which there is a need for a kind of infinity, a vessel containing everything that a person can be, the essential source from which the "man" of man and God and law comes. The goal here is not to define a single God or cluster of gods, and certainly not to have to choose One or the other; rather, it's to imagine a kind bottomless well from which a person gathers all that they are and all that is around them, and then does the work of making sense of what this endless spiral means.

In this chapter, all eyes are on memory, specifically on how Dylan gathers, assembles, modifies, and represents texts as an expression of divinity, infinity, and transcendence.

Bob Dylan is a scavenger, a collector of shards of lyrics, poetry, art, literature, film, popular phrases, and sacred words repurposed as songs.

His techniques press hot-button topics in our time—appropriation, plagiarism, cultural borrowing and stealing, and the nature of genius and innovation. And at the same time, whether he knew it or not when speaking to *Rolling Stone*, Dylan's way of working as a songwriter dates back to the artistry of the sages, poets, and rhetors of the classical world—the world of Pompeii and even a thousand years before. This makes him the most important contemporary inheritor of the cluster of memory techniques that have sourced and saved great ideas for millennia. His artistry in weaving of new patterns out of the memory of what has come before also offers a profound lesson in balancing spiritual continuity and disruption.

I will take a different view of Dylan's context in Chapter 7, depicting the social and mythic landscape of America as another kind of infinity. If Dylan's version of the art of memory offers a boundless palette of colors from which to choose, America is the canvas upon which he paints his sprawling vision. Through memory and through America, Dylan touches upon what Jewish mysticism calls the *ayn sof*, or limitlessness of a universe that exists beyond anything our minds can conceive. We work in this realm of the infinite and we can feel its energy and power, but it's more than we can ever truly understand.

In Chapter 8, having tried to grasp the divine landscapes of Dylan's work, we will stand—inevitably—before the Law. There I will expand and sharpen conclusions about a life of the spirit that Bob Dylan may be suggesting for his or any contemporary journey of purpose, from the most fundamentalist worldview to a dreamy mysticism carrying the seeker beyond the material world. Then Chapter 9 lays out an exercise imagining the world after Dylan—and may it *not* come soon—in which his legacy and the broader story of the rise and fall of the Rock and Roll Empire will continue to influence the musical and spiritual universe chapter and verse for years to come.

Now, where were we again? Right. Memory. The art of memory, which is Dylan's textual palette and something very much like being planted in the mind of God. Glad I remembered that. Onward.

Simonides Has Left the Building

The art of memory is a system of mnemonic tools that can shape the composition of every kind of art or story. The popular conception of how creativity manifested itself for ages was "from inventory comes invention," and "re-membering"—or putting together the members of ideas, phrases, or any artifact from one's cultural warehouse—is what the ancients meant by "creativity." They understood the world of ideas and texts as if it was the periodic table in chemistry. Maybe there are only 118 elements, but the skillful combination of the right ones can produce anything.

In the classical world, the same concept held for the realm of the intellect. While the raw materials a creator could obtain and employ were finite—shards of poetry or liturgy or philosophy or legend, just like Dylan collecting inventory from his contemporary Pompeii—the possibilities for combining these elements in new ways were infinite. Canonical works like The Odyssey and the New Testament relied on a sophisticated set of memory practices ensuring access to the raw material that combined with an assembler's equally strong sensibility of how to reshape it, how to build or rebuild a world.

Part of Dylan's power as an artist emanates from the discipline and playfulness embedded in his use of the art of memory. First, he has agency, a very strong sense of his creative self. This gives him permission to remake the world based on the reflection he draws from it. "These people that you mention," he sings in "Desolation Row," a song re-membering an entire culture, which we will listen to closely shortly, "I know them, they're quite lame. I had to rearrange their faces and give them all another name." Always gleaning and re-membering something new from what he has heard, seen, collected, and stored, Dylan's art of memory draws a direct line from the classical world to classic rock, and from classic rock to spiritual wisdom.

Dylan has often been compared to Homer and Shakespeare, but if we want to juxtapose Dylan with a poet of the past, particularly a poet from the classical world, comparing Simonides and Dylan is compelling too. Here are two poets memorializing and renewing the cultural rubble that society might otherwise leave behind so that society can see itself for what it really is.

In a well-traveled story related by the Roman rhetors Cicero and Quintilian, the poet Simonides (ca. 556–469 BC) had been invited to perform at a large banquet in honor of the wealthy nobleman Scopas. Think of it as a corporate gig, the kind of show for a private, establishment audience that poets of old and rock stars of today take on to keep revenue flowing. Simonides's job was to massage the ego of his host with songs of praise composed especially for the occasion.

Before we get too far into the story, we should be clear about how "true" it might be. Like urban legends distorting the facts of events that have taken place in the life of someone famous—such as Dylan's motorcycle crash, which was variously said to have been staged or caused brain damage or killed him—there is a kernel of truth imbedded in what has been passed down concerning Simonides and the banquet.

That crash did completely disrupt Dylan's public career, though no one has ever fully confirmed its factuality. No one is sure how much of the tale of Simonides describing the origins of the art of memory is true either.

There was almost certainly a poet by that name, and there surely was a poetic technique prominent in Simonides's era to which he and others subscribed. People cared about this technique. They wanted to know how it worked and where it came from. Maybe there really was a catastrophe like the one that Simonides is said to have witnessed. At whatever the level of truth of each strand of the story might be, like the art of memory itself, a legend woven by a skillful storyteller comes together in a pattern of fact and embellishment that people need to hear. Regardless of where the kernel of truth lives within the details of the story, the tale of Simonides is designed to explain the genesis of one aspect of the art of memory vividly—a quality essential to the art of memory itself. This weaving of fact with legend as a way for society to deepen its understanding about something that makes it tick will come to be part of the role that contemporary musicians play as well.

Such factual fluidity is a prime element of classical rhetoric. Another is at play as well. Call it the technique of teaching values and ideas through stories of the rock stars of the classical world, the way that a celebrity can stand for a whole school of imagination if they star in the right legend. Explaining an important concept through the presence of a single charismatic person simply makes the topic more resonant.

The technical term for this kind of story is a *chreia*, an anecdote crafted about a person that carries an important message transcending the protagonist. In the same way that the legend of George Washington cutting down a cherry tree embodies the value of honesty or Abner Doubleday's revelation of the game of baseball epitomizes a treasured sense of the essence of America, Dylan's stories of locking eyes with both the wrestler Gorgeous George and Buddy Holly teach the importance of a disciple's inheriting tradition from a master. These are all *chreia*, traditional ways of inculcating values through a story.

So here comes Simonides, a poetic hired hand, in a classic(al) rock-star story meant to teach us about the art of memory. He sings for his supper, concluding with his poem. Then his patron Scopas—like the club owners who led Chuck Berry to insist that he'd only play if paid in cash before the show—tells him that he will give Simonides just half of his fee. Someone informs Simonides that two men are waiting for him outside. He makes like Elvis and leaves the building, but there is no one waiting for him. With Simonides next to the banquet hall, the roof collapses, killing Scopas and all his guests. When the friends and relatives of the dead arrive later to collect the bodies of their loved ones, they find them so disfigured that they cannot identify who is who. Simonides, however, recalls the place where each of Scopas's guests was seated at the table and identifies them all.

By Accident

This legend claims that by accident—an actual, horrible accident—Simonides discovered the "method of loci," one of the mnemonic techniques of the art of memory. If the creative act of the art of memory Dylan calls upon is rearranging faces and giving them all another name, Simonides models what comes first: being able to store the intimate details of a society's "faces" in careful order in a specific place so that they can be identified, explained, and reimagined in a way that makes sense when this inventory is needed most. How this technique of visualization in the art of memory intuitively lives alongside many other mnemonic devices in Dylan's work goes a long way toward explaining the impact of the best of rock and roll on general culture, as well as Dylan's pivotal role in bringing ancient and contemporary worlds together so that popular music mattered so much.

The method of loci calls for exacting visualization of specific locales, which are then used as templates for storing and remembering information. Just as Simonides instinctively used the fixed tableau of a banquet table to place and recall the names and faces of the scores of guests at Scopas's feast, people employing the method of loci "place" or "store" information, such as the words of a speech, piece by piece in different locations throughout a meticulously crafted, unique, and unchanging background constructed in each rememberer's mind.

This tableau might be a perfectly reimagined banquet table, as was the case with Simonides, or the rooms of one's childhood home, a main street, or any other stable and intimately known space. In fact, one of the reasons why people often have dreams that take place in their childhood home is because the unconscious is naturally drawn to an emotionally resonant, unchanging background for its playful reworking of the order of the world in the eyes of its beholder.

With each word or image marked like a treasure in a familiar place—a house, a street—only the rememberer holds the map. When a person needs access to the knowledge stored within the tableau, they take a "stroll" through the mind to "re-collect" and "re-member" the words, plucking out what is on their mind like clusters of flowers planted in a lush private garden. Though such a system might seem counterintuitive, the method of loci was as commonplace in the ancient and medieval world for encrypting information into fixed grids and matrixes for later recall as the hard drives or clouds we use to store information today.

While the description of Simonides's "discovery" is almost certainly an apocryphal *chreia* for teaching a system developed by many people over a long period of time, it claims a singular role for poets still applicable today: poets use powerful tools of memory and communication to make sense of the world, particularly in times of crisis. They know where society's most important secrets are hidden, especially when the world gets a little shaky—or worse, when it falls apart, like in the throes of a pandemic when finding stability and survival become one and the same.

When people are confused about who is who and what is what and they can't even identify the people they love, rich memory channeled by the poetic arts matters most. In this context, Dylan's explanation of his creative worldview in the aftermath of 9/11 is even more poignant. This also highlights the importance of Bob Dylan's asking his audience, for this and all the reasons, "How does it feel?"

As the culture of the 1960s pulled many longstanding societal assumptions apart, people needed a poet to sort through the rubble and point in the right direction. At first it might have looked like one big party—a banquet of the who's who, like the one Simonides attended—but things got serious. And that's the story of memory, salvation, and popular music. It's no wonder that a generation that embraced the symbolism of a "rolling stone" bumping along wherever nature or fate would take it also wanted someone to stop the motion and establish roots or dredge up some collective memory to get grounded in something greater than what individuals might access alone.

This wisdom remains relevant, even essential, particularly with the new varieties of uprootedness of our own day. It's not just the disembodied nature of life's moving online as accelerated by COVID-19; it's also the fracturing of our physical communities along the lines of identity, race, sexuality, and religion, which Dylan has been describing for decades. Memory is our common inventory, and it's more fragmented than ever. What music can still do to close these societal gaps is important in equal measure because music, poetry, art, and narratives grounded in common inventory still have the power to teach and heal.

Praying with "Tumbling Tumbleweeds"

As reflected in his remark to Mikal Gilmore about the ancients, the central figure in Bob Dylan's body of work has always been a solitary seeker narrating a life-stroll through the United States of Pompeii. His songs are glimpses into a journey through gaps between what has been upended, what is otherwise frozen in time, and what needs to be explained. While Dylan's role as an artist reflects the archetypal task of the poet as personified by the figure of Simonides, the memory system Dylan employs is not as rigid as that of his forebear, who captured in his mind only the images of the elite faces around the table at a rich man's feast.

Dylan suggests other tableaux for memory, songs laid upon a rotating backdrop of lyrical vessels such as a window, a street, a hotel room, or a parlor. The content tripping in and around these tableaux consists of the flotsam and jetsam of the lyrical vocabulary of traditional post–Civil War folk, blues, country, and art songs from the heyday of recorded music, leading up to the Depression and into Dylan's boyhood in the 1950s; cinema from silent to noir to Westerns; literature and poetry across genres; old radio and television shows; the Bible; and layers of mythology.

The raw material of Dylan's songs is like the catalog of the New York Public Library, where, as we will see shortly, Dylan claims to have had a creative epiphany that set the course of his vision of salvation in America. The songwriter's imagination spirals meaning from their inventory, like a preacher spinning a sermon out of a collection of verses. Pieces of a cultural puzzle are configured and reconfigured, each song a "re-membering" encounter with the canon out of which the story of a hero's salvational quest unfolds.

"These old songs are my lexicon and prayer book," Dylan told *The New York Times'* Jon Pareles in 1997. "All my beliefs come out of those old songs." Dylan has explained how he works with this vast catalog piece by piece. "Well, you have to understand that I'm not a melodist," Dylan said to Robert Hilburn of the *Los Angeles Times* in 2004.

My songs are either based on old Protestant hymns or Carter Family songs or variations of the blues form. What happens is, I'll take a song I know and simply start playing it in my head. That's the way I meditate. A lot of people will look at a crack on the wall and meditate, or count sheep or angels or money or something, and it's a proven fact that it'll help them relax. I don't meditate on any of that stuff. I meditate on a song. I'll be playing Bob Nolan's "Tumbling Tumbleweeds," for instance, in my head constantly—while I'm driving a car or talking to a person or sitting around or whatever. People will think they are talking to me and I'm talking back, but I'm not. I'm listening to a song in my head. At a certain point, some words will change and I'll start writing a song.

This repetitive pattern of "meditation" leading to new work is familiar to any committed musician, the jamming and woodshedding of repeating scales and riffs, a familiar rhythmic phrase, or a favorite song that ultimately bends itself into a melody that is called "new," even if its creative genetic code can be traced back to an original, older form from which it organically emerged. Though this repetitive practice takes place in garages from Olympia to Boston and in jazz clubs and in the locked bedrooms of teenagers everywhere, Dylan is also describing an art of composition used by bards going back to ancient times.

A family heirloom bible is passed down, dog-eared with notes on the family tree from generation to generation. It's a sanctioned weaving of time-honored words and phrases that have been repeated by ancestors for hundreds of years, but also a private history lying upon the kitchen table or nightstand, as familiar as a great-grandmother's watch or a baby blanket cherished over generations. So too are these traditional songs. Dylan's grasp of both the spiritual gravitas and the familial comfort of the memorial cycle of song captures what must have drawn him, like a moth to the flame, to the traditional music he carried into pop.

One of the most compelling studies of the art of repetitive, formulaic, meditative musical-poetic composition appears in the scholar Albert Lord's *The Singer of Tales*, an attempt to explain how it was possible that Homeric epics—some of which are well over ten thousand lines long—could have been memorized and performed orally by the bards of ancient Greece. Lord maintained that singers, performers, composers, and poets in traditional cultures create an original though inherently formulaic lyric every time they performed. They do not repeat a text verbatim, having memorized it "word for word." Rather, each performance is comprised of a performer's reworking of a shared body of modular, traditional formulae within deep structures of action and narrative common to their culture.

Think of how the basic narrative of a myth like that of a great flood grips cultures across the globe in local iterations, or a charmed warrior like King Arthur or Gilgamesh exists with similar diversity. A person well versed in fairy tales or mythology, even if they have not heard a particular version of a tale before, can fill in the details of a new version within the genre because a prototype already lives deep within their cultural memory. While the names and places and emphases of the story change based on the locale of the storyteller, its "hero-ness" or "flood-ness" stays the same, just as anyone familiar with the twelve-bar blues structure can finish a line with the right feel and technique once a first lyric has been dropped and the music begins to unfold. This is one of the reasons why *The Iliad* and *The Odyssey* follow predictable epic narrative patterns and are full of stock characters and repeated epithets, like "rosy-fingered Dawn" and "gray-eyed Athena," that serve as signposts, basic riffs of the repertoire, to help the bard stay within the traditional form.

Having grasped both the deep narrative structure and the catch-phrases and formulae of the genre after years of listening to masters, a bard does not recite a text from memory. Rather, the bard activates his ability to access all he has heard recited before him, the "performance notes" he has gathered over years, laid out in various orders in a Simonides-like tableau in his head, creating his own traditionally grounded but original performance as he sings and plays.

A virtuoso rock guitarist can sit in with any band anywhere. The same is true with even more sophistication in the world of jazz, which parses a core melodic narrative remembered over and over again through a conversation of improvisation. A classic bard too is essentially sitting in on an entire world of phrases and stories when telling his own tale. The more he listens to other bards, the tighter his system of memory becomes. The more he practices by telling his tale, the richer his own expression will be. And while we are focusing primarily on lyrical memory, as Dylan's description of "Tumbling Tumbleweeds" affirms, melodies are just as formulaic and fluid as words, a flow of sound carried by musicians across time, remembered and adapted as it is heard and played, tune leading to tune from a common ancestor like the descendants of a family carrying that heirloom bible together through life.

Where Have You Been?

With obsessive, attentive, meditative listening and repeating, Dylan has gorged himself on every kind of music. And being the very hungry listener, reader, and just plain observer that he has always been, he has gobbled up just about every other form of cultural content as well.

The "tumbling tumbleweeds" just tumble across the landscape until they become something else: "At a certain point, some words will change and I'll start writing a song." The result—musically, lyrically, and thematically—is a reworking of a kind of memorial of inherited content placed upon the tableau of a song. In some sense, Dylan has sat in with all the worlds of expression that challenged and excited him and then transformed these traditions into something else. He has re-membered culture and preserved it by metamorphosing it. This is one of the reasons that Dylan's work has entered so deeply into people. It is familiar and new at the same time. It is from everyone and from a private place in someone's own head. Like a second mind or collective consciousness individuals tap into in their own unique way, this stream of songs succeeds in being both intimate and shared at the same time.

And this too is one of the secrets of the appeal of rock and roll and popular music as a whole. Clearly a societal disrupter by every measure, it is also a chain of tradition—seen and unseen—with maps of familiar creative territory continually morphing into new expression, a creative movement of call and response, its dynamism held gently in check by both choices and mysteries of continuity.

Blowing up pop the same year that his namesake died, Elvis Costello was an anti-Elvis, but his name was still Elvis. Pat Smear was the guitarist for the L.A. punk pioneers the Germs, whose wild front man Darby Crash killed himself just hours before John Lennon was murdered. After Crash's death, Pat Smear went on to join Nirvana. Nirvana loved the Germs, but it too disbanded when its lead singer, Kurt Cobain, killed himself, and Smear joined its successor band, the Foo Fighters, now flagbearers not of the hardcore punk where Smear began but of what's left of the mainstream rock and roll it was meant to overthrow. This dynamic between continuity and disruption among popular music's characters and heroes is, of course, present in its content as well.

Dylan's work is loaded with examples of both conscious and unconscious continuity and change in content. Christopher Ricks[31] and others note how "A Hard Rain's A-Gonna Fall" comes out of the deep structure of the Scottish ballad "Lord Randal," itself part of a particular song pattern reaching back hundreds of years. The traditional ballad says:

O where have you been, Lord Randal, my son?
O where have you been, my bonny young man?
I've been with my sweetheart, mother make my bed soon
For I'm sick to the heart and I fain would lie down.

And what did she give you, Lord Randal, my son?
And what did she give you, my bonny young man?
Eels boiled in brew, mother make my bed soon
For I'm sick to the heart and I fain would lie down.

What's become of your bloodhounds, Lord Randal, my son?
What's become of your bloodhounds, my bonny young man?

O they swelled and died, mother make my bed soon
For I'm sick to the heart and I fain would lie down...

Dylan says:

Oh, where have you been, my blue-eyed son?
Oh, where have you been, my darling young one?
I've stumbled on the side of twelve misty mountains,
I've walked and I've crawled on six crooked highways,
I've stepped in the middle of seven sad forests...

Oh, what did you see, my blue-eyed son?
Oh, what did you see, my darling young one?
I saw a newborn baby with wild wolves all around it
I saw a highway of diamonds with nobody on it...

And what did you hear, my blue-eyed son?
And what did you hear, my darling young one?
I heard the sound of a thunder, it roared out a warnin'
Heard the roar of a wave that could drown the whole world...

Professor Ricks—in a style so full of intelligence and humor and with such a complete command of the subject matter that his explanations themselves are a kind of epic tale—traces parallels, allusions, interpretations, and plain old playfulness between Dylan and scores of texts of the Western canon, from the Bible to Yeats, with a chorus of voices across eras along the way. Jenny Ledeen, a marvelous character who has traveled the Dylan circuit in the summertime with a trunk full of copies of her book *Prophecy in the Christian Era*,[32] cites meditative parallels between Dante and Dylan, and Dylan and the Bible.

Examples of Dylan's practice of repeating "old" material in order to produce "new" material abound because this is exactly how Dylan, as a traditionally grounded poet and musician, works. As he says himself, Dylan is not a melodist, but that does not mean he has not pulled and plinked his way to many wonderful melodies. He's a rememberer, a transmitter of tradition, a keeper of cultural records even as he crafts their representation through his own imagination—disrupted, continuous, playful, communal, and also fully his own microcosm of the mind of the divine.

Dylan Is a Fake

Commenting on the apparent overlap of phrases from Dylan's 2006 album *Modern Times* with the works of the somewhat obscure 19th-century poet Henry Timrod (known as the "poet laureate of the Confederacy"), singer-songwriter Suzanne Vega pecked at Dylan's art in an op-ed in *The New York Times*: "Did he do this on purpose?" she asked.[33]

> I doubt it. Maybe he has a photographic memory and bits of text stick to it. Maybe it shows how deeply he immersed himself in the texts and times of the Civil War, and he was completely unconscious of it...In other words, is he really "a thieving little swine," as one "fan" puts it? Well, I guess he is. But I am trying to imagine a Bob Dylan album with footnotes, asterisks, "ibid."s, and nifty little anecdotes about the origins of each song. It's not going to happen. He's never pretended to be an academic, or even a nice guy. He is more likely to present himself as, well, a thief. Renegade, outlaw, artist. That's why we are passionate about him.

Across the country at the *Los Angeles Times*, Joni Mitchell said, "Bob is not authentic at all. He's a plagiarist, and his name and voice are fake...Everything about Bob is a deception."[34]

(I and many more would like to know what exactly Bob Dylan was doing with a Confederate poet. This parable remains unexplained.)

A fake, a thief, a deceiver. All varieties of sleuths have been trying to crack Dylan's codes since the beginning. His first official biographer, Robert Shelton, claimed that Dylan "exploded with anger" and went "underground" in 1964 after the major periodicals broke the news of Dylan's "true" identity as Robert Zimmerman. In the latter half of the 1960s, A. J. Weberman claimed to be the founder of "Dylanology" as well as a wider science he called "garbology." A self-proclaimed Dylanologist, Weberman specialized in deciphering the hidden meaning of Dylan's songs, which often happened to coincide with the songwriter's secret messages to Weberman himself.

DJ and sleuth Scott Warmuth is an eminently skilled Dylanologist. Even if this title carries some ignominy, when it comes to Dylan's art of memory and the questions of fakery and genius, Warmuth is definitely on to something—maybe even everything. He takes apart the entirety of several Dylan albums as well as his quasi-autobiography *Chronicles* and demonstrates, fairly unequivocally, that Dylan has taken a basket and collected scraps of words and images, pieced them together, and represented them as his own. Warmuth meticulously tracks each cut and paste, not only sourcing the content Dylan has used as the raw material for his work, but also cracking the code imbedded within— the hidden trails of thought, inside jokes, and messages for the most discerning listeners or readers about what is really happening in the music and words. Dylan is revealed as a text collector and a text shapeshifter and assembler as well.

At first blush, it might seem that all this talk of begging, borrowing, and stealing from other sources is a bit of a cheap shot or worse. Isn't the ever-praised Bob Dylan supposed to be a genius creator, struck by inspiration in the middle of the night on a tour bus or in a hotel, cigarette in hand—bringing down to earth some emotional lightning that gets bottled into a song. Is he a copycat, a curator, a hustler, or all of the above?

The truth is that the truth is far from that. For one thing, texts are, by definition, a form of recollecting—both recollection as memory and re-collecting as in gathering items from the lost and found. The truth is that this is how much of human language works, inside and outside of art. Someone must have given us those ABCs we are using to make sense of these sentences. It's good that we have repurposed them together. We all learn to speak by listening and imitation and trial and error, reaping and reshaping what we have heard until we find ourselves saying things all by ourselves.

When someone is upset and their partner says they sound just like their father, it is not only because of the tone of their voice, it's because they are using a sentence—or parts of a sentence, or words and phrases—they heard their father say (or yell, actually) without even knowing it. Indeed, the Latin root of the word "text"—*textus*, for those keeping score at home—actually means something woven, like a web or a basket. Texts are consciously formed structures for holding something all in one place. Texts, like Dylan's songs, hold an otherwise unwieldy array of words, phrases, allusions, jokes, rumors, prayers, and television ads that the composer has collected and carried around and now comes forward to share with everyone else.

More Love, More Theft

The novelist Jonathan Lethem, a fine listener not only to Dylan but to pop culture generally, wrote a piece about Dylan's "plagiarism" in *Harper's*[35] following the controversies that Suzanne Vega and Joni Mitchell commented upon in relation to the album *Love and Theft*, an album we will listen to differently in the next chapter, which focuses on America and race. Lethem's piece about Dylan and plagiarism, crafted in his signature lit-pop voice, mixes eclectic references across many genres, the prose crackling. And then, in the final portion of the essay, Lethem reveals that the entire essay is cribbed—mostly word for word—from pieces that other people have written.

Curation and creation, working hand in hand, are issues of consternation and contempt today, but in the world of classical poetry that Dylan repurposed for rock songwriting, reworking the past was the essence of the creative act.

Whether it is his adaptation of William S. Burroughs's "cut-out" approach to composition, the good creative luck he earned by investing in building an inventory in order to "invent" songs, or a conscious laying of hints and codes, Dylan reshapes inherited content. He is a preacher entering a theme affirmed by and embellished with the content laid upon it, in the same way that the art of memory includes the method of loci (Simonides's banquet hall), the laying down of pieces of text collected in a visual stroll, and the vivid and at times grotesque images monks inserted into medieval manuscripts to mark or trigger junctures of particular importance.

The architecture of Shakespeare's Globe Theatre was designed to reflect the image of a perfectly tuned mind. So, too, Dylan's work depends on many iterations of the broadly defined category of memory. Researching it too closely or calling upon too much Dylanology for the scientific explanation of the work does not do justice to the majesty of the art. If it's said that the universe was created by words, and that God got to create the words *and* the world—"God said, "Let there be light; and there was light"—and then everyone else's creativity and creations depend on editing those words that were left, holy Mad Libs forever, a divinity game of memory for all.

At the end of a piece on the Grateful Dead's "Uncle John's Band"[36] that claims a direct link (or set of direct lifts) of lyrics maneuvered by Dylan onto *Love and Theft* via the New Lost City Ramblers—traditionalists of Greenwich Village who stayed "folk" while Dylan went rock—Warmuth quotes the Ramblers' leader, John Cohen. "The study of folklore," Cohen said, "is not simply to preserve the past, but to make the present more comprehensible."[37] This alchemy of past to present is how societies in the dark see themselves in the mirror an artist holds up during the light of day. But the comments of Joni Mitchell and Suzanne Vega suggest that some of us in modern times or, rather, postmodern times, may not have the patience to accept this approach. The idea that individual brilliance depends on serving the past pushes the limits of what we generally expect creativity to mean in a world where everyone is a genius creator in training, a smartphone universe in the palm of their hand.

The line between copying and creating is fine indeed. Consider Jonah Lehrer, a high-flying postmodern writer, banging out hyper-clever articles in hip magazines, and then a book on all the intelligences that animate the virtual world of networks and nanoseconds of synapses and associations characterizing communication in a World Wide Web world. Unfortunately for Lehrer, he got caught making up quotes attributed to Bob Dylan in a book about genius that his publisher was forced to shelve. He was not punished for lifting content from vast troves of unattributed phrases in his memory or dog-eared copies of obscure books or Bob Nolan's "Tumblin' Tumbleweeds." Without any context or content to mold, he simply made things up and claimed they were real. Lehrer did not bend facts and legends to his will as artists do, but invented facts and legends to fit his narrative.

This is the subtle difference between fakery and the art of memory. The intentions of memory may be good or they may be bad. After all, as Suzanne Vega says, no one has ever claimed that Bob Dylan is a nice guy. But the assumption of the classical poet was that knowledge reworked to suit the mood of a room, song, speech, or dream was the poet's highest form of expression. Can you take what we all should know and enlighten us beyond what we already know? Have you tilled the fields of culture long enough to ensure that something new will grow from it?

This fine line between making something new out of something old and making something up highlights a paradox concerning authenticity, both back in the day and in our day as well. I have already suggested that by making *himself* up, sorting through all manner of masks and allusions of self to shape his persona, Dylan somehow comes to be seen as a figure who embodies generational values of "going your own way" and "doing your own thing."

He was from the beginning of his career a kind of patron saint of authenticity. Does authenticity mean being a distinctive individual with a new way of being in the world, or creating oneself in a respectful revival of the past based on what one has learned and remembered? If the secret of authenticity is the latter, it would seem to require humility to hold the whole enterprise together. Humility is a trait prized by all great religious traditions but harder to come by in the rock and pop universe. To lean into the past means to lean *out* of oneself. To be real and authentic is to recognize one's limits and open up to let the world flow in. Again, Dylan's creative practice offers a hint about a deeper spiritual truth.

Memorial Culture

"Desolation Row" is the finest example of Dylan's use of the art of memory to make something new in the world out of something old. Here, science, legend, sacred text, show business, and literature circa 1965 meet with Cinderella, Bette Davis, Romeo, Cain and Abel, the Hunchback of Notre Dame, the Good Samaritan, Ophelia, Einstein, Robin Hood, Dr. Filth, the Phantom of the Opera, Casanova, Nero's Neptune, the *Titanic*, and Ezra Pound and T. S. Eliot, "coming to the carnival tonight" on Desolation Row.

Understood as a modern-day use of the method of loci, the figures and things of the song emerge in a fixed geographical tableau, the
imagined thoroughfare of Desolation Row, a street whose emotional
value gives it the "stickiness" classical teachers demanded for their students' memory landscapes. It's a place with an emotional pull as Dylan's
narrator walks through a series of invented scenes dictated to himself,
"re-membering" or putting together cultural content from everywhere.
It's an entire world of the familiar controlled by the choices of the
rememberer. The imagination of the poet with the best memory gets to
control the world.

Picture the scenes of "Desolation Row" as a massive baroque painting in a cavernous ivory hall at the Metropolitan Museum of Art or
the Louvre to gain a sense of how a poet takes possession of cultural
content, reworking and reorganizing material to create a memorial in
the same way that the great painters populated the walls and ceilings of
cathedrals with mythic tales containing their own revisions (and reser-
vations) about the sacred canon. Just as Simonides grabbed the social
elite in the steel trap of his mind so that their faces might be preserved
and reintroduced when the time was right, the storyteller of "Desolation Row" slowly unburdens his memory of faces when he needs to call
for the world. But unlike Simonides, who claimed to match the map
of the people at the banquet precisely, Dylan employs an aggressive
form of the method of loci, applying his own unique order to the raw
material of history because this is the only way that tradition can make
sense to him. He reorders the canon, history, and life itself so that he
can survive them:

Yes, I received your letter yesterday
(About the time the doorknob broke)
When you asked how I was doing
Was that some kind of joke?

All these people that you mention
Yes, I know them, they're quite lame
I had to rearrange their faces
And give them all another name
Right now I can't read too good
Don't send me no more letters no
Not unless you mail them
From Desolation Row

The letter he has received—perhaps the motivation to which the song, as a whole, responds—is an artifact from before the poetic salvation of the reimagined life of Desolation Row. In fact, this letter may as well have been written in another language altogether. It is unreadable, even offensive, because it ignores the fact that only reconstructed reality can preserve a sensitive soul from the cultural chaos of the "real world." Dylan's narrator sees the same faces as his pen pal, but each with "another name," planted within his personal grid of desolation, grounded in the only terms that he can understand and accept.

In that same revealing Mikal Gilmore interview cited earlier and subsequently, Dylan, when asked if he had a message for people after 9/11, quoted the Rudyard Kipling poem "Gentlemen-Rankers": "We have done with Hope and Honour, we are lost to Love and Truth / We are dropping down the ladder rung by rung / And the measure of our torment is the measure of our youth / God help us, for we knew the worst too young!"

Dylan goes on to say: "If anything, my mind would go to young people at a time like this. That's really the only way to put it." Empathetic and intuitive, he believes that truth-telling (and truth-shaping) visionaries can expect to face loneliness and rejection in their society. In a sense, this is what makes them feel very old, but it also allows them to identify so cogently with the predicaments of the unknown facing the young. No wonder "My sal-*VAAAY*-tion" is Dylan's abiding goal. And it's no wonder he could use some relief.

Fittingly, the word "desolation" comes from the Latin word "*desolare*," meaning "to forsake." Dylan literally sees his generation forsaken, frozen and dead, forcing him to create a new matrix for living. Despite its dark side, the reward for carving new cultural paths can be freedom and lucidity that hints at transcendence. These are potential "paths to salvation" that Max Weber hinted were bound to come even when rock and roll was just a glimmer in his proto-postmodern eye at the beginning of the 20th century. And then it happened.

In Dylan's vision, making sense of the world, reworking its traditions and reporting back on what he has seen, is a story of life and death, because—as Dylan has made clear for himself—life is about being born and born and born again, a kind of transfiguration.

Mary Carruthers, author of *The Book of Memory: A Study of Memory in Medieval Culture*, describes the phenomenon of "memorial" culture in the realm of medieval monks. From the time of Simonides through Cicero and onto the stages of the Church fathers and medieval monastic culture, the method of loci served as a basis for sacred arts of meditation, prayer, translation, and manuscript production grounded in reworking and relearning classical, inherited texts.

Ostensibly the monks of medieval times created nothing "new" for generations. Picture the ink-stained hands of silent figures in brown and gray robes meticulously crafting tomes containing psalms composed a thousand or more years before, adorning them with miniature gold-leaf images of gargoyles and birds and flowers—people dedicating their lives to relaying traditions without "inventing" anything. The was nothing "new" except for the very inventory that was the basis of cultural reinvention and rebirth in Europe during the Renaissance. Simply holding on to an inventory and working at keeping it fresh can be as revolutionary as any amazing "new" idea.

Hear Dylan repeating an old country music phrase in his head while you think he's talking or singing to you—until that very old tradition evolves its keeper's experience into something new. Memorial culture, like the monastic life, is a constant process of resurrecting societies' dearest inherited figures and symbols in study and art, "making present the voices of what is past," as Carruthers wrote, "not to entomb either the past or the present, but to give them life together in a place common to both in memory."[38] Truth be told, this is the story of classic rock stations, too, where no song was composed earlier than thirty years ago, yet somehow, people long to meditate upon them and glean meaning and excitement from the same tunes again and again.

Carruthers affirms that a creative act in the ancient and medieval world was not an event of invention ex nihilo but an act of re-imagination—the reconfiguring of texts and images preserved by the monks in the various tableaux of their memory so that they could form new sacred content out of inherited material that would otherwise have been lost and left for dead. The holy trade of Carruthers's monks was to give life to tradition by preventing it from dying. This sounds like something of a godly act—or at least a partnership in something godly. And it seems that Dylan, who speaks of the music he loves as his lexicon and prayer book, must feel the same way.

Three People to Do That Job

While it may be considered lowbrow by rock purists, Don McLean's "American Pie," featuring a very familiar jester, offers perhaps the most widely known ode to the rock and roll pantheon. It works because like most epics, it finds longing and sweetness in the throes of heroes' both falling and escaping youthful death and dying. The punch line of "American Pie" is ironic considering that it was released in 1971, an era in which the music it mourns was a dominant cultural force. Music had not died. It was growing exponentially. Nonetheless, McLean puts the pantheon into motion to interpret a new-old story where music defines consciousness and meaning as well as loss. It's a peppier, poppier, but also sadder version of "Desolation Row." Inspired by a plane crash in 1959 that killed first-generation rock stars Ritchie Valens, the Big Bopper, and Buddy Holly, "American Pie" parses rock and roll history as a lost Garden of Eden, a long and winding road of an answer to questions of loneliness, longing, and death.

In form, "American Pie" is a collection of charged symbols, audaciously lengthy for a song seeking radio play. Even after Bob Dylan had shattered radio's three-minute standard for rock singles with the six-minute cut "Like a Rolling Stone" in 1965, DJs in 1971 still needed to flip the 45-RPM single of "American Pie" to play the second half of the song. Lasting almost eight and a half minutes, it remains the longest recording ever to top the *Billboard* Hot 100. This alone indicates the cultural resonance of "American Pie," though now, sadly, its resonance for an entire generation or two of pop-culture consumers is a series of films about a bunch of kids at Ritchie Valens's forever-age with only one thing on their minds. On a jukebox in a bar, on a radio in a car, or behind the door of a bedroom, this rhyming ballad punctuated by a rousing singalong chorus has demanded and received an unusual amount of affection and curiosity from several generations of listeners who pass ultimate judgment on what voices are memorialized and preserved.

McLean wrote an ode describing the relationship of each remembered figure of the all-time rock and roll banquet to a core tragic event. For *The Iliad*, the orbit of all meaning was the bloody conflict of the Trojan War. For "American Pie," it was the violent death of three rock prodigies in a frozen North Dakota field. Alluding to everyone from the Beatles and the Rolling Stones to Elvis and from Bob Dylan to Jimi Hendrix to Janis Joplin to the Monotones, "American Pie" suggests that spiritual exile for singers and fans alike was inevitable after the Big Bang-like blow of that plane crash.

As his litany reaches its conclusion just before a slow-tempo repetition of the final chorus lamenting rock and roll's demise, McLean eulogizes Valens, Bopper, and Holly as akin to the Holy Trinity. Once the body of this divine trio has died on Earth, only a mundane world clouded by illusion remains. (As I have mentioned before and will mention again, Dylan claims Buddy Holly made fierce eye contact with him from the stage at the very concert that preceded Holly's death.) It is a world without magic where even giants stumble in the dark.

McLean has been reticent to discuss the literal meaning of the song for decades and often refuses to play it—though he recently sold the original handwritten lyrics for more than a million dollars, claiming that his descendants did not quite have a "mercantile spirit" and needed the money. Whether the Holy Trinity of exile embodies the original form of the popular godhead topped by Buddy Holly or other suggested interpretations, such as John Kennedy, Robert Kennedy, and Martin Luther King, Jr., or the three members of Holly's band the Crickets, reference to the Holy Trinity of the Church grounds rock and roll in a mythic cultural landscape in which music is a direct reflection of one of the most significant religious or mythic structures of the past two millennia. Later, we'll hear Dylan use Jesus on the cross as a metaphor for all of America. In that case, however, it takes a nation itself dying for the music to live.

Popular musicians love dipping into an inventory of ancient symbols like the Trinity as they craft an attitude of cultural antiauthoritarianism or gravitas. But any calling upon of the Trinity cannot be passed over lightly. At home in liturgy for millennia, the Trinity also lives a rich creative life in the gospel, folk, blues, and country music out of which rock and roll emerged. Rock inherited from core sources of American music a comfortable and even intimate relationship with sacred symbols. Images of Jesus—or Moses or the Apostles or Adam and Eve or Abraham or Ezekiel's Wheel or nearly any major biblical trope—travel from the earliest recorded music of the 20th century to Mother Mary in the Beatles' "Let It Be" and Jesus in the pronto-punk dreamscapes of the Velvet Underground or to the post-punk irony and despair of the Vaselines, as made famous by Nirvana's *MTV Unplugged* cover of "Jesus Doesn't Want Me for a Sunbeam" just before Kurt Cobain became yet another rock and roll messiah tragically styling his own pop martyrdom.

"American Pie" is but one example of how Dylan's approach urges music to mythologize itself. It's clear from the many "conversion stories" told about Dylan—those stories of the first time a major artist heard Dylan and it changed their creative life—that he opened artistic minds to a new way of re-membering the world. Despite her critique of Dylan, Joni Mitchell was also a convert. She said:

> Just a simple thing like being a singer-songwriter. That was a new idea. It used to take three people to do that job. And when I heard "Positively 4th Street," I realized that this was a whole new ballgame; now you could make your songs literature. The potential for the song had never occurred to me—I loved "Tutti Frutti," you know. But it occurred to Dylan. I said, "Oh God, look at this." And I began to write. So Dylan sparked me.[39]

Jimi Hendrix, who revolutionized rock as a guitarist from worlds no one had even known about before, let alone visited, credited Dylan with inspiring the core of his vision. "Dylan really turned me on," he said in March 1968. "Not the words or his guitar, but as a way to get myself together."

Re-Meet the Beatles

And then we meet the Beatles. Look at how the album cover of *Sgt. Pepper's Lonely Hearts Club Band* allows the Beatles to shape, question, interpret, and master cultural meaning with a single photograph that serves as a gateway to their music in one of rock's greatest years—1967. The cover of *Sgt. Pepper's* places the Beatles in the center of a landscape composed of figures ranging from Marilyn Monroe to Karl Marx, Carl Jung to Shirley Temple, and Laurel & Hardy to Dylan Thomas. Interestingly, Jesus was originally slated to appear in this collage. He was removed after John Lennon's suggestion a few months earlier that the Beatles were more popular than their almost special guest and actual protest pyres of Beatles albums burned back in the USA.

Rock and roll interpretation thrives on both provocation and ambivalence, tinting vision and image with a distinctly outsider's point of view. On *Sgt. Pepper's*, like the Roman god Janus, the presence of the Beatles is two-faced. In one image they smile in the brightly colored band uniforms of their *Sgt. Pepper's* alter egos. In the other, stationed within the very same landscape, their eyes downcast and skin gray, the band looks somber, even dead. Whatever this dichotomy says about the Beatles' self-perception in 1967, their stance at the center of a pop-myth tableau models how rock and roll seeks the images society cares about, gathers them, plops its own face right into the center of the universe of a self-curated pantheon, and then lets its iconoclastic spirit animate and define this amalgam of reality. Like oracles and prophets of old, musicians assemble and interpret the mythic and cultural material unleashed by society and recast it in search of insight and understanding. And because rock and roll lives and breathes emancipation, deconstruction and disruption are often the places where building consciousness with these tools begins.

While there are many examples of how the music of *Sgt. Pepper's* interacts with its cover art—which quickly became an archetypal image for pop culture as a whole and should be traced right back to Dylan's "Desolation Row"—let's consider only one: "She's Leaving Home."

If the inherited world of symbols and meaning brought together by the Beatles on the cover of *Sgt. Pepper's* creates "two-faced" ambivalence inducing either the gift of life or the specter of death in its messengers, this is merely a creative reflection on a social-mythical level of the ambivalence of typical young people who embraced the Beatles as meaning-makers. "She's Leaving Home" describes its heroine's well-meaning parents snugly asleep during their daughter's dark night of the soul. When they awake to find her gone, having been unable to express why she had to leave, they cannot understand why their child would abandon a life so carefully built for her.

Just as the Beatles of the album cover question whether their era's cultural inheritance is either trouble and treasure, the home of the family in "She's Leaving Home" is broken precisely because the generations living in it cannot agree whether their home gives life or takes it away. Here, as in mystical traditions across cultures, creation contains upper and lower realities. The godhead, the gods, and the heroes of scripture and myth wrestle with the same jealousies, ambitions, and imbalances as humans of the earth. Similarly, in "She's Leaving Home," a common domestic story is wrapped in the album cover's depiction of the essence of what shapes the apex of world culture. Big and small stories combine to thicken the meaning with which the Beatles want their audiences to grapple.

Once Dylan made rock stars his age's prophets and seers (and yes, it was he who turned the Beatles on to pot in the mid-sixties; then came the flood), they did not only channel and interpret cultural meaning. They also chose ways to model it. So beyond the languages of composition and songwriting, performance and image, the Beatles publicly embodied—and *still* embody, since, like gods and heroes, rockers on the level of the Beatles have shelf lives that allow them pretty much to last forever—the cultural myths and dichotomies that *Sgt. Pepper's* explored continued long after the band had broken up. Each member of the band remained a star in his own right, and each somehow represented a different approach to the generational gap and cultural tumult they had earlier exposed—both because they did, but also because, in the same way that worshippers provide part of the character and shape of the gods they worship, we needed them to be that way.

Ringo Starr, one of so many pop music figures to use a stage name packed with meaning to shape his persona, from Elton John to Joan Jett, let the good times roll, partying through the changes and cultivating the persona of a lovable man-child unsullied by the cultural fray. Paul McCartney dug deeper into pop melody and craft and remained miraculously spry as a performer, but became less and less identified with work pursuing social meaning. George Harrison sought and taught spiritual transcendence and higher purpose beyond material dilemmas, emerging as rock and pop's most well-known spokesperson for the practices and wisdom of the East. And John Lennon, who maintained the pace and presence of a rocker for the first half of the 1970s before finding refuge in family life in the five years before his murder, continued to disrupt and challenge just about everything in the cultural milieu.

Lennon's song "God" from *John Lennon/Plastic Ono Band* (1970) concludes with a litany (or perhaps a liturgy) of mythic and cultural figures in which he *does not* believe, painting a soundscape not unlike the visual landscape of *Sgt. Pepper's*, but disrupted with even more mythic clout and punkish disdain. All is God and all is challenged as a deceptive landscape of illusions that must be exploded for the cause of truth. Like *Sgt. Pepper's*, "God" convenes a mythic pantheon. But here Lennon's perception of its meaning carries no ambivalence. Buddha, kings, and Kennedy, Elvis and Dylan, and even the Beatles themselves are name-checked and are said not to be worth believing in, let alone following.

Even as the waves brought forth from the cultural explosion of rock and roll continue to sound the shore, Lennon rejects them all, and all that is left to believe in is himself and his Yoko—a home, which is in and of itself an ironic return to the form of domesticity disrupted in "She's Leaving Home" just a few years before. And then, truly as if it is an enactment of a Greek tragedy or a biblical parable, the week that Lennon returned to the pop arena with a new album entitled *Double Fantasy* in 1980—the "two faces" of life as a Beatle dating back to *Sgt. Pepper's* still reflected in the title—he was shot to death by a fan for whom a rock star's impact on reality/double fantasy was so great that voices had convinced him to kill the messenger.

Just as they have always been in religion and myth, death and rock and roll memory are very much entwined. But not only did Dylan survive his dance through rock memory and myth physically and creatively—perhaps because Holly died for his sins, as marked by that stage-level stare?—he lived to see countless songwriters, from Don McLean to Joni Mitchell, take permission from his groundbreaking approach concerning what a pop song could do in order to shape a new canon for how people saw the world.

There is no "American Pie" without Dylan, and maybe no *Blue* either. He broke the sound barrier of what popular music could say and do, and then, because of songs like "American Pie"—a eulogy for an entire nation sung by a musician not much more than a kid himself at the time—it's impossible to imagine the American landscape without the demands made upon it by popular music. As Dylan taught it to do, rock mythologizes itself from the moment of its arrival. It races toward death, stares it in the face, mourns and longs and spits and scowls gigantically, and also asks whether—by the way—it can live forever in its own epic stories of itself.

In its adaptation of the art of memory, popular music finds a way to live intimately with myth, as music stars like Dylan embody both the voice of the muse and the spirit of gods and goddesses. Ridiculously dramatic and self-important as they may be, at times outdated and arrogant and boring and boorish in ways that rightly outraged the punks—who invented their own gritty myths and rituals by slaying the myths of their predecessors—the classical element of classic rock stars provides listeners with generative meaning and comfort. A classical cultural essence allows us to ride the waves of something greater than ourselves, guided or inspired by figures that resemble us, and to sense purpose beyond what we know, to feel the buzz of living in the presence of something eternal.

These are deep human needs in all societies driven by any kind of religious sensibility. Popular music brings mortality, eternity, and destiny to life for us in our cars or in the privacy of our homes or in a stadium surrounded by eighty thousand souls communing with the same mythic groove. This embodiment of the ethereal is for us, as it has always been, as essential a nonmaterial need as anything humans know, and the entire process depends on the art of memory, curated skillfully by a poet who knows how and what to remember, and then how and when to help us understand that we remember much more than we think we do, maybe even everything we need to know.

In memory, the entire universe lives, and this—for a concept all but impossible to understand—is as close as we can get to experiencing something like the embodiment of God. As a seeker of salvation with deep faith in music and text, Dylan immerses himself in tradition, all possible paths of man and God and law contained within. The result is unfiltered intimacy with the vocabulary of timeless questions, a poet stationed at a window on Desolation Row calling upon the eyes of the world to gaze upon the frozen days of Pompeii below and report back on what he saw—which includes everything and everyone that he or anyone else has ever seen.

7. America

He said his name was Columbus, I just said, "Good luck"

Washington is not a place to live in. The rents are high, the food is bad, the dust is disgusting, and the morals are deplorable. Go West, young man, go West and grow up with the country.

So said journalist Horace Greeley in 1833.

The 19th century was a bloody age for American mythic advancement and ruthlessness. Native peoples were slaughtered as a nation stretched itself from the Atlantic to the Pacific. Gold rushes produced pop-up towns that disappeared seemingly overnight. The violent, backbreaking, unrelenting labor of slaves, former slaves, and immigrants resulted in a network linking together the country from the Gulf of Mexico to Canada and from the old East all the way to the pastures of Stanford University, whose founding father Leland Stanford drove the final stake of the First Transcontinental Railroad into the ground.

It was a wildly expansionist age, swirling with movement, time leaping forward. This is a nation that begins a century with George Washington's successor John Adams as president and ends with Teddy Roosevelt in the White House. The distance covered in these one hundred years in terms of geography, technology, politics, and culture are cavernous, almost unimaginable.

Think of open spaces, of venturing outside of oneself or one's community to seek a home. The 19th century was defined by fierce energies for wrecking, building, restoring, celebrating, or rejecting the need for a direction to that home. But above all, this was an age and a nation defined by slavery.

Much of this chapter revolves around the Dylan claim—which I will cite in a moment—that the national, spiritual lesson from which he learned the most is found in the story of America and race. If America is the landscape, the mythic context for Dylan's exploration of faith and salvation in which the art of memory provides the texts, then slavery and race are the fault lines running between man and God and law within that landscape. Music is called upon to map these divisions, and perhaps to heal them. This story, imbedded in Dylan's story, of risking everything to make it home takes on particular intensity in the 1800s, when so much of what shapes the boundaries and limits of America come into being.

There's No Place Like Home

Back in the mid-19th century, after the word of God first came to him in Hudson, Ohio, the town of his birth, John Brown spent time in Kent, in what had been the Connecticut Western Reserve, America's first Wild West, now the Rust Belt—as in Kent State and that bloody song "Ohio" that Neil Young penned in a night and released within a week a century later. Brown came to understand that God wanted him to dedicate his life to ending slavery, and that he should be ready to die for it, which eventually he did.

While it wasn't quite a shot heard 'round the world, when John Brown took guerrilla warfare and fire-and-brimstone political persuasion west to Bleeding Kansas in 1855, it was Kansas's civil war that had begun to expose fully the bleeding edge that Bob Dylan called America's original sin, the all-encompassing template of his lyrical, mystical vision: slavery. It was this wound that would soon nearly cause the entire country to bleed out, then only less than a century old and just about to face its ultimate schism. Like a deep laceration that would not close and heal, the eternal infection and inflection point of slavery would continue to flare up and endanger the United States' body politic continually.

Kansas *was* the west of "Go West" in the days of John Brown—"Go West," like a former president's signaling "YMCA," serving as the title of a post-folk, post-rock manifesto of gay liberation by the Village People—not a flyover state. To finally fulfill his prophetic mission, John Brown, who was already not a young man, headed back east from Kansas to Virginia and Harpers Ferry in 1859. When they caught him after the raid he led to shake slaveholders to their senses, two of his sons dead, Ralph Waldo Emerson said of Brown that he would "make the gallows glorious like the Cross." This is a phrase that rings true with Dylan's conceptions of the formative period of history in which Brown lived as well as Dylan's creative, historical mindset sifting through old newspapers in the New York Public Library later in this chapter. But before we get there, let's stay in Kansas a bit longer.

"What's the matter with Kansas?" This was the question asked by Thomas Frank's 2004 bestseller. The state served to measure a state of permanent dis-ease in America even in Brown's day, offering an overture to the Civil War. Kansas had been invited to join the union but had to make a choice about slavery before closing the deal. It was split right down the middle, blue versus red, pro-slavery versus abolitionist, Border Ruffians versus Free-Staters. And everyone, as a Midwestern singer would sing a century later, was sure that they had God on their side.

Way out west on the new frontier, where so many had gone to explore or build or escape, Kansas just couldn't make up its mind—just like much of America today, a century and a half later—about which side of history it wanted to be on. The choices seem so obvious it's not clear how they could ever beg a question, but somehow, devilishly, the question remains just as open as it was back then.

In Kansas, when Auntie Em and Uncle Henry's people were just establishing their homestead, Dr. Brewster M. Higley wrote the lyrics for the poem "My Western Home" in 1873. This was eight years after the end of the Civil War and the assassination of Lincoln, in the midst of Reconstruction and the planting of the poisoned seeds of Jim Crow. "My Western Home" would become Kansas's state song. The lyrics should ring a bell. "Oh give me a home where the buffalo roam…" it begins. Would this openness invite generosity and empathy or make for a deadly trap for those for whom the God of the history of the West was *not* on their side?

Questions of home and oppression—whose is it, where is it, how do you build it, how do you get there, and how does it feel there?—challenge the essential paradox of America, that home on the range, that row of houses where you need to rearrange your neighbors' faces and give them all another name. Wanting to understand the home of self and soul in and of America motivates Bob Dylan. These questions orient his work to a national-personal dilemma he parses time and time again, and it goes like this: "How does it feel to be on your own, with no direction home?"

Goodbye, Columbus

When Bob Dylan began seeking "road maps for the soul," he turned his creative gaze to America. As it did for Gwendolyn Brooks and Oliver Stone and Barack Obama, the contours of America provided a durable yet malleable mythic vessel, one rich in history, still in motion, and also thoroughly infused with homegrown music and words pulsing through it.

In *Chronicles: Volume One*, Dylan describes a scene at the New York Public Library during his early days in Manhattan. Dylan's American intellectual journey was just beginning, and interestingly enough, it required him to leave the heartland for what was arguably the nation's furthest cultural fringe in his day, Greenwich Village. Yet his most potent enclave for adventure was in his imagination, his mind, which sought to plumb the gaps where history had meted out time. Whether embellished or factual, Dylan's visits to the library are an example of a Dylanesque self-made *chreia*.

I talked about the use of this Greco-Roman pedagogical device in a previous chapter, an exemplary statement about or by a person embodying values that epitomize their mission. Dylan's library *chreia* is another link in this self-created man's bonds of creation, gently pulling his audience's chain as link follows link and inventory begets invention.

As a reverie about how he spent his afternoons before passing the hat and grabbing a hamburger at one of the coffeehouses while learning to ply his trade as a folk singer, and whether it is factually "true" or "false," the intent of the tale is as all-encompassing as the formative American reality of race it describes.

Dylan writes:

In one of the upstairs reading rooms, I started reading articles in newspapers on microfilm from 1855 to about 1865 to see what daily life was like. I wasn't so much interested in the issues as intrigued by the language and rhetoric of the times...Back there, America was put on the cross, died and was resurrected. There was nothing synthetic about it. The godawful truth of that would be the all-encompassing template behind everything I would write.[40]

Like Emerson, framing the Civil War with the religious iconography of a nation's crucifixion, death, and resurrection, Dylan claims an unavoidable mythic calling that leads him on a pilgrimage into the nexus of man and God and law that slavery haunts. According to Dylan's description of that "godawful truth," confronting the legacy of slavery is as essential to his work as chasing the whale is to Captain Ahab or coming home to Penelope is to Odysseus.

Dylan traces the fault lines and fissures of slavery within the crux of man and God and law as a new member of a profession with expertise in the appropriation of Black culture for making both money and meaning. Amidst rebooted demands for Black liberation coalescing in Black Lives Matter, there are few cultural mirrors better than music for witnessing the triumphs and tragedies of the conflict Dylan claims to have absorbed between the stacks of the library. If popular music punches its creative ticket on themes of emancipation, how its artists relate to the divide between white and Black is an essential litmus test of who is and is not doing the work of man and God and law.

For Dylan in particular—as for rock and roll, as for popular music, as for America—the expression of a white artist dependent on Black music is a more concentrated way of asking how to be *any kind of American* without fully acknowledging slavery as the spiritual and economic engine driving the birth of the nation.

These are white people's problems—to have the choice to ask how does it feel, or to *just not feel* regarding the legacy of slavery; if there is wisp of creative life or death for those who are drawn passionately to Black music, this is nothing like an actual brush with death in the form of living with racism, or carrying the burden of ancestors who were slaves. As a white artist and white person, Dylan tries to address these gaps. But his musical calling does not merely provide an "all-encompassing template" for his own creative and spiritual reflection. He also demands over the course of his career that any form of American spiritual wisdom face the legacies and burdens of slavery, the Civil War, and race. In the ecosystem of man and God and law, Dylan's creed assumes that "man" means people of every color or background. This should be a given after hundreds of years, but it's not.

Where Many Martyrs Fell

The original Greek meaning of the word "martyr" is "a person who witnesses or testifies to an event or idea." In early Christianity, and in parallel beliefs in Judaism and across the Roman Empire, martyrdom came to mean sacrificing one's life as an act of testimony.

This pattern recalls one of the cluster of Bob Dylan's songs about dreams—"Bob Dylan's Dream," "Series of Dreams," "Bob Dylan's 115th Dream," "'Cross the Green Mountain," and many more. Dreams imply a brush with truth both outside of oneself and deep within, a message above and below the surface of things catalyzed by a force seen in a fleeting glimpse. These dreams often involve historical figures suggesting a spiritual perspective that leaves the singer made aware of something new—woke, you might even say—when he awakens from the dream.

As we have already heard, when it comes to martyrdom and testimony, as deeply as Dylan's narrator in "I Dreamed I Saw St. Augustine" enters a salvational drama, he holds a sad complaint: he cannot be a martyr. Augustine taunts the dreamer, "tearing through these quarters in the utmost misery." These quarters, all four of them in fact, are once again the dreamer's heart. Dressed in gold, a religious icon animated in real time, Augustine strikes at the "gifted kings and queens" who, despite all good intentions, cannot attain the ultimate gift of salvation—not even with a figure of religious greatness in their midst. The dreamer's soul "already [has] been sold," and he is condemned to isolation and inaction.

Bob Dylan, as we know from sometime around his 115th dream or so, is not Abraham Lincoln. Nor, as we will hear shortly, is he JFK. And though Dylan is obviously not MLK either (though perhaps a bit like Martin Luther), the values and metaphors of some of his most famous "pointing-finger songs" reflect tropes from the most famous American dream of them all, Dr. Martin Luther King, Jr.'s "I Have a Dream" speech on the steps of the Lincoln Memorial in 1963. Despite utterly different life experiences, a fair portion of King's gospel and Dylan's blues link back to many of the same African-American textual and sonic sources.

To finish this list of what Dylan is not and to return to dreaming, Dylan isn't Joe Hill either, even though the melody for "I Dreamed I Saw St. Augustine"—an example of the previous chapter's art of memory, or artful stealing, depending on which side you're on—is a knock-off of the melody and structure of the song "I Dreamed I Saw Joe Hill Last Night." This folk standard popularized by Pete Seeger and Paul Robeson serves as a kind of ongoing musical visitation by the itinerant Swedish-born Wobbly activist and singer Joe Hill, who was executed in 1915 on murder charges, likely as a result of his activism. As any folk-singer-school dropout like Bob Dylan would know, Joe Hill was a figure of martyrdom for the labor movement.

When it comes to martyrs who haunt his musical dreams, Dylan has a lot to say, a lot to feel, and—based on the topic's returning as often as it does—a lot to live up to. This results in lyrics betraying self-judgment and disappointment. His narrator in the song "Jokerman" sings of being a friend to those who give their lives for a cause, but his interest in the ultimate human sacrifice is more than social. It is essential, a standard for purpose he holds as high as anything, to which, as described quite vividly, he comes up short.

Looking at themes of teachers and death previously, martyrdom is a thread woven through the fabric of faith and salvation that covers Dylan's songs. Let's recall yet again a Black figure like Hattie Carroll as well as Emmett Till, Davey Moore, Nettie Moore, and Rubin "Hurricane" Carter (who was imprisoned but not martyred in jail) entering Dylan's repertoire. And, of course, Dylan spends a tremendous amount of creative and spiritual energy probing the meaning of the myth and mysteries of the martyrdom of Jesus of Nazareth.

One figure of destiny stands out in a crowded dreamscape of martyrs. That's the namesake of the song "Blind Willie McTell." This is a tale of that all-encompassing template of slavery wrapped up in "Like a Rolling Stone"'s ever-present demand for a Romantic American witness to explain to his audience "how does it feel?" in that song's chorus. Here, a white singer plumbs the interminable gap between being a secondhand witness to the "sad complaint" of slavery and actually being a martyr because of this original sin.

Recorded during the period of 1983's *Infidels*, "Blind Willie McTell" appears publicly a decade later as part of the first official installment of Dylan's *The Bootleg Series, Volumes 1–3: Rare & Unreleased 1961–1991*. For years fans have wondered why this song, which is considered a masterpiece, did not make the cut for the album itself. This was not the first or last time Dylan chose not to include stellar work on an album, another interesting riddle of how Bob Dylan manages his own talent.

The *Bootleg Series* recording of "Blind Willie McTell" is spare—a vocal, piano, and acoustic guitar soliloquy placed lyrically in an upper room at the ethereal St. James Hotel, that infamous blues infirmary by another name. Looking out the window to gaze as far back as he can to trace the blues, Dylan sees barges crammed with people stolen from Africa, bodies chained, people suffocating and separated from loved ones, sold, degraded, and worked to despair and death. This is the story a singer like Blind Willie McTell—whom Dylan's most determined biographer, Clinton Heylin, suggests may in fact be a placeholder for Blind Willie Johnson[41]—inherits for American song.

The singer is framed in front of the same window he gazed through crying in "I Dreamed I Saw St. Augustine," an observer watching and feeling mythical history unfold even if he is removed from it. He witnesses everything, time itself breaking down. But as we recall that the original meaning of martyrdom is to witness an idea or value through the sacrifice of one's own life, the best Dylan can offer is a respectful, even magisterial imitation of those who suffer all around him. Despite all the love he affirms for the people and culture resulting from America's formative myth, Dylan's song of slavery is still just "love and theft."

We are left with a haunting, unfinished mythical and musical hall of mirrors. America, having died on a cross, is carried away by angels of song. Their voices echo salvation, but these sounds are like a rumor Dylan once heard, another one of those fleeting, inside-out dreams in the night. He can try to get a message through about what this all means, but he's limited, quite literally pale by comparison in relation to the voices of the blues he has blended into his own—maybe lovingly, maybe respectfully, and surely for the fluid ways of folk music which he drove to extremes—from the sources he steals.

But a challenge remains, maybe an insurmountable one. If rock and roll tragically and suffocatingly squats to a large extent, like America, on the landscape of slavery, how can an American musical prophet, false or true, serve as an honest broker for righteousness while still acting out the scenes of an American crime? And if his knowledge of what really happened in that long, dark night of the national soul is once, twice, or even three times removed, what's it really worth?

American Tunes

The great songwriters of the rock and roll era after *The Freewheelin' Bob Dylan* learned from, were inspired by, and in some sense used Dylan's inventory for their own invention. Most were trying to understand how to feel about America too. This included those born or working elsewhere. At its core, even when it is nurtured abroad, particularly in the UK, rock and roll is an American art form with American questions baked in. Rock's artists have, since the beginning, drawn maps of American imagination and myth in their own exile on main street, though bands like the Kinks—even more so and better than the Beatles—described the intimacies of middle-class life in Great Britain for a global audience as well. As a movement, rock tried to make sense of what it heard in the echoes of the ghost ships Dylan saw and the change Sam Cooke promised would come.

Chuck Berry traversed "The Promised Land." Joni Mitchell traveled with other pilgrims to "Woodstock" then on to "California" and "This Place." Bruce Springsteen sought a reckoning from the time he was "born to run" to the anger of being "born in the USA" to both escape and resignation on the more recent *Western Skies*. "An American Band" passed through every Ticketmaster town on the Grand Funk Railroad line. A band called America tried to do just what such bands do. Green Day one-finger-saluted the "American Idiot" nearly a generation after Kim Wilde's "Kids in America" jumped up all over MTV. New Dylan #136 or #142, John Cougar Mellencamp, spied "Jack and Diane" all dressed up with nothing but their chili dogs in their hands. Even the uniquely awful Kid Rock made his suburban white claim for the trope of the American Dream as the vehicle of rock and roll had run out of gas, crashing into Childish Gambino's fierce "This Is America" and Taylor Swift's glassy-eyed, derivative "Last Great American Dynasty." All these artists came to look for the same place Paul Simon simply called "America."

A dreamy kid on the bus, passing time with his lover and in his own reveries, Paul Simon took to American exile in London in 1965, just a year before Jimi Hendrix did the same at a critical career crossroads. Simon was far away from home, not sure of where he belonged or what he wanted. Maybe he would go law school, he thought in deliberations reminiscent of Lou Reed, who worked for his father's accounting firm for a year after the Velvet Underground went asunder, prior to David Bowie's drawing him back into the rock and roll ring.

A sense of exile sharpens the creative edge and is often crucial to an artist's finding the means to tell a story of their homeland. Neil Young, Joni Mitchell, and Leonard Cohen all wrote their finest musings about Canada while living elsewhere. James Joyce was exiled from Ireland so that he could reimagine it in his fiction, and James Baldwin, an expat for years, was one of America's most eloquent critics.

Living in London as his songwriting vision coalesced—and during the same period Bob Dylan was launching the rock and roll triptych that began with *Bringing It All Back Home* and included visits, tours, and relationships in the UK—Paul Simon encapsulates in "America" a post-Beat and cusp-of-the-hippies wanderlust for finding the heart of a country. He carries a songwriting cross of spiritual restlessness that defines the baby boomers, rock's core fan base, all the way to quests and questions in much more comfortable circumstances (and supported by South African musicians) on the album "Graceland" much later.

In 1973, nearly a decade after his sojourn in London and long departed from Art, Paul Simon the songsmith, the pro's pro, revisited the theme of America, an American dreamer still dreaming. It's often late in the evening or early in the morning in Paul Simon's best songs, but the capstone of "American Tune" is what makes Paul Simon such a creative force: he is a worker who tirelessly writes and edits—a legal pad a song, he says—at times *too*-perfect work. It may be late for America, he sings as its bicentennial nears, but it's still not too late to work on it—in song. Like in his composition "Jonah," Simon isn't swallowed by a whale like the biblical prophetic exile. In America, Simon is engulfed by music. But that does not make him a martyr. Just like the biblical Jonah, he survives, tucked in tight, protected by his song rather than the giant fish, alone in his thoughts, plugged into his higher powers and his work. Challenged as he may be, he's safe.

The Living Will Take It to Heart

Dylan does not seek that kind of comfort. He doesn't want to be swallowed up by anyone or anything. In a practical way, he simply keeps moving. His Never Ending Tour is not limited to America, of course, but few if any performers have made as many whistle stops in the USA as Dylan, who could have rested on his laurels decades ago. This is a tack taken by a very different adopted New Yorker, John Lennon, the same figure whose death punctuates the end of Simon's "The Late Great Johnny Ace" in 1983, a reflection through the window of his time in London, bearing certain resemblances to "Blind Willie McTell." In "The Late Great Johnny Ace," the legend and history of two Johnnies collapse into a single tragic narrative, bookends of rock and roll mortality.

Bob Dylan and John Lennon had a prickly relationship. George Harrison and Dylan are said to have been very good friends, and who doesn't love Ringo? Dylan has said that he considers Paul McCartney a talent that no one, not even he, can touch. It's also clear that without Dylan, "I Want to Hold Your Hand" would never have metamorphosed into "She's Leaving Home," and that the Beatles, along with the Beach Boys, probably encouraged Dylan to "go electric" as much as anyone.

John Lennon lived several musical lives before he took to nesting in the Dakota on New York City's Upper West Side to raise a child for five years out of the public eye. It was a period not unlike Dylan's self-removal from performing beginning in 1966. Then, as we heard previously, just as Lennon released *Double Fantasy*, a batch of new songs, in 1980, he was murdered most foul. "Roll on, John"—echoing "The Late Great Johnny Ace"—Dylan sang decades later on *Tempest*. There are all kinds of martyrs in America. A song could not protect any of them.

Dylan's tool kit for mapping America does not rely on topography, though rivers and mountains and unique characteristics of cities and towns are all part of his poetic template. His instruments of measurement are musical. As he talks about music in interviews or his writing or the occasional much-ado-about lecture, we hear how music (and, to a notable extent, literature) provides the cartography to help him navigate the issues that have troubled him since those early days in the New York Public Library. Tying all these themes and purposes up in a single epic, reflective of many epics more, results in "Murder Most Foul," a tale of martyrdom and a hint of salvation through the songs of the empire. But before turning to 2020's "Murder Most Foul," we need to return to Paul Simon's "America" for one more moment of comparing two American musical masters.

Simon's songs "America," "American Tune," "Jonah," and "The Late Great Johnny Ace" are high points of the genre of American musical seekers, weaving in the longing, exile, and musical obsessions heard in "Murder Most Foul" as well. But these roadmaps for the soul of "how does it feel?" do not speak of martyrdom. And this is a clear difference between Dylan's musical spiritual wisdom and that of other songwriter peers.

Dylan calls upon a kind of gravitas and mythic framing that leaves the songwriter—and perhaps the audience—with nowhere to hide. He seeks the fault lines between life and death, and he also feels some form of national fault. There is a price to pay in those divisions. Simon wants a solution, just like the biblical Jonah, who was so distraught that God forgave the people of Nineveh for their sins. Stay under this castor oil plant, God said to Jonah. My ways are way above your pay grade. There are things you cannot know about the long arm of the divine law and the extent of divine mercy. Jonah does not like this answer, but he's a worker, not the boss. He will need to keep his head down. So, too, Paul Simon accepts the blessing and curse of mysteries beyond himself and covers himself in his art.

The same is true of Bruce Springsteen, whose contribution to American popular culture is large. But when the pressure was on, he chose, at a peak moment of American crisis after the storming of the Capitol on January 6, 2021, to offer an ad for Jeep, a Super Bowl Sunday plea for a middle ground in the middle of the country—at a tiny church in Kansas, which is no place and every place like home as mentioned earlier—with soft dirt in his soft hands and an actual cross centered in the frame. He was panned for giving such easy answers in a time of deep spiritual unrest in the land, and rightly so.

Dylan wants something else, not the comfort of Simon's craftsmanship inside of the song, like a shipbuilder building a vessel for stormy mythic seas, nor the easy out of the muddled and middling common denominator Springsteen proposes. Dylan wants to tell us about the wound. His spiritual wisdom echoes not Jonah but Ecclesiastes, said to have been written in the final phase of life by a wizened King Solomon. By the time of his composition of Ecclesiastes, Solomon had seen and done it all—building the Temple, cavorting with a thousand wives, and knocking out both the Book of Proverbs and the Song of Songs while he was at it. "Better to go to the house of mourning," says Solomon, "than to go to the house of feasting, for that is the end of all men; and the living will take it to heart" (Ecclesiastes 7:2).

In the first chapter of his analysis of Bob Dylan's canon through the lens of the seven deadly sins, Christopher Ricks writes:

> The claim in this book isn't that most of Dylan's songs, or even most of the best ones, are bent on sin. Simply that (for the present venture in criticism) handling sin may be the right way to take hold of the bundle.[42]

Something similar could surely be said here. All the themes in this book are just that—ways of grasping in a useful way the meaning embedded in the work. The intent is not a restrictive view, not one that has to be just right, or even has to be right. The goal is to take hold of something that matters and really sit with it so that it can do its work that needs to get done.

In this particular case, thinking about America, about martyrdom, we see time and again how Dylan seeks out sin and pain. And then, as an artist at least, in the spaces between repentance and release, he chooses resignation. He wants to open these spaces—call them wounds—even further; to call them out, to probe them, and to document these spaces for all the world to see. He'll happily make the shoes, walk the walk, talk the talk of the dark places—as close to a martyr as one can come without going all the way home. *Chreia* or a tall tale, wishful thinking or just showing off, Dylan puts his money where his mouth is when it comes to taking the American story of martyrdom seriously in ways that none of his rock and roll musical peers can really touch.

Odysseys and Ends

"Every telling has a tailing and that's the he and the she of it." So wrote James Joyce, exiled Irish master, in *Finnegans Wake*. Mythologist Joseph Campbell cut his academic teeth on the study of *Finnegans Wake*, Joyce's final explosive work, published at the start of World War II. A favorite of both the Grateful Dead and *Star Wars*'s (and perhaps more important for our topic, *American Graffiti*'s) George Lucas, Joseph Campbell synthesized mythological themes that make themselves at home in the art and expression of thinkers across the landscape of contemporary culture work whether they know it or not.

An author of many books, Campbell was made famous through a series of discussions with Bill Moyers on PBS series called *The Power of Myth*. He popularized the term "monomyth," but this was actually

Joyce's coinage, right there in *Finnegans Wake*, describing the archetypal plot serving as a kind of scaffolding for the collective unconscious. The monomyth is a singular, universal narrative arc followed by Odysseus and Huckleberry Finn and Sethe from Toni Morrison's *Beloved*. A cycle of a birth, calling, discovery, battle, glory, and death common to all heroes, the monomyth also tracks to mystic psychoanalyst Carl Jung's template for the cycles that any human soul must travel.

The monomyth is, above all, the story of bringing one's soul and self back home to share something with the world. And getting home, at least in Dylan's words, has been his destination all along. "I was born very far from where I'm supposed to be," Dylan says in *No Direction Home*, Martin Scorsese's 2005 documentary about his early years as a recording artist, "and so I'm on my way home."

The playing field for this odyssey—personal, creative, political, musical, and mythic—is America, because this is the place that Dylan most observes outside of himself. When he told his fans and followers to "be observant" at the release of "Murder Most Foul" in a tweet that blazed across the ether, Dylan drew our attention to the knot of self and country, another shot at a direction home when there seems (still, crazily, after all these years) to be no clear path to get there.

The name of the game in America is getting around the horn and touching home base. Just like the game that was known for a century as America's favorite pastime, baseball, the goal is making it home. Or consider passing "Go" in one of the nation's other classical pastimes, Monopoly. Here, if you work hard and get a little lucky, you can buy a house (or even a hotel), but by game's end, the only players who survive are protected on a corner in some orderly neighborhood categorized by color.

America is a home on the range that imagines itself as a level playing field not unlike a geometrically secure game board of Monopoly or the holy diamond of the old ball game, just one field for Blacks and another for whites until Jackie Robinson—who literally had to *steal home* at Ebbets Field, which was razed so that the land could host a public housing project after the Brooklyn Dodgers themselves headed west—broke up the party on summer days that kid Dylan could have heard for himself with his sacred music on the family radio. Like the Negro Leagues or the blues, America hides its multitudes, for discovery by the extra curious or the outcast outside of the lines. It loves to speak in platitudes about amber waves of grain and purple mountain majesties from California to the New York island, but its greatest artists—Mark Twain, Ethel Waters, Maya Angelou, Philip Roth, Bob Dylan—have conflated the multitudes of self and platitudes of country grandly to remake the rules for both.

Understanding Dylan and his work in context of the American story, there's no avoiding the multitudinousness of it all, and there's no avoiding jumping back and forth like Walt Whitman between country and fantasy, personal and collective, mythic, lyrical, pseudobiographical, and historical, as Dylan has done all along.

As in the Best It Is

Is America a utopia or a scam? A dreamy landscape of discovery, a refuge, a new start—or a place to hide? A ghost ship? What is America? Where is it and who holds the map to find it, to navigate it, to know where it's headed?

At a moment of national agony, two months before the murder of George Floyd during an arrest on suspicion of passing a counterfeit twenty-dollar bill in Dylan's home state of Minnesota as COVID-19 was laying the world flat on its back barely a round into the fight—Dylan's statement in "Murder Most Foul" weaves together mourning, resignation, and that all-encompassing template of mortal sacrifice to revisit his favorite themes.

Choosing a single song to sum up Dylan's epoch of American creativity is impossible. His work spans many styles. It has its share of masterpieces as well as its share of false starts—likely true for any prophet, false or otherwise. There are many patterns of song structures, cycling iterations of tricks from the American songbook, some of the oldest of them made new, and a cluster of songs that introduced new chapters for what pop songs could do. But in the long list of contenders for the title of best in class, a strong case can be made for "Murder Most Foul" as Dylan's most compelling American masterpiece.

"Stay safe, stay observant, and may God be with you": These are the words on social media that announced the release of "Murder Most Foul" in March 2020. "Stay safe," Dylan said as COVID-19 was rapidly incapacitating the world, the United States alone on a course for nearly six hundred thousand dead at the time of this writing. "Stay observant," he said as the federal government misdirected attention from addressing a massive human tragedy. "And may God be with you," he said, words like the final utterance of the captain of a ship about to go down.

The song itself was recorded just a month prior to its release and written some time earlier, though Dylan has not said when. "Murder Most Foul" is a memory stroll, directed but easy, very observant indeed, like the walk of memory in the realm of the art of memory we have already stepped through, a series of reflections and collections of cultural artifacts re-membered and reordered by the narrator. The melody is almost flat, a trope akin to the recitation of a sacred text, but in a major key, the time signature loose, the accompaniment atmospheric, with arpeggio-style piano, percussion, and an occasional overlay of violin.

Anchored in the events of the day of the murder of JFK, "Murder Most Foul" is a reverie, not a narrative, reminiscent of parlor songs like "Tryin' to Get to Heaven," where the singer daydreams at dusk or in the early morning hours in the stillness of a quiet room, maybe staring again out the window of the St. James Hotel, a lamp or two lit, his voice tracing the steps of a mind wandering with soulful intent but no particular place to go.

While Dylan may have bumped into the phrase "murder most foul" in the 1964 film of the same name based on Agatha Christie's *Mrs. McGinty's Dead* or even the 2018 episode of the television show *Vikings* carrying that title, the genesis of this line is act 1, scene 5 of William Shakespeare's *Hamlet*. Here the ghost of Hamlet's father rises to reveal that he died in his bed at the hand of Claudius, his brother, now the king of Denmark. His death, Hamlet's father tells his son, was a "murder most foul." The ghost shocks the prince, who had no inkling that his father was assassinated by his own kin. Incitement toward revenge, it seems, underlies the dead king's revelation, and this changes the course of Hamlet's remaining days. Now he must decide whether and how to avenge his father.

By the end of the play, only Hamlet's friend Horatio survives to tell the tale. Horatio, who arrives from Wittenberg University, Martin Luther's alma mater, where he and Hamlet studied together, may symbolize the shift from old-world traditional culture to new-world rationality that marks trends that plant the seeds of the Rock and Roll Empire sussed in chapter 2. Once Hamlet decides to heed his father's call, battling insanity and inaction, everyone else in Hamlet's circle but for Horatio—including Hamlet—will be dead.

All the elements we have heard in the American tunes we have listened to thus far resonate in "Murder Most Foul." JFK is a martyr felled by dark, powerful forces, making the narrator a kind of redux of Hamlet, and maybe even making all in Dylan's generation who looked to JFK as a father figure a kind of orphan. However they relate to President Kennedy, the singer of the tale and his audience share the center of a drama of longing and witnessing. Dylan peels the lyrics of "Murder Most Foul" from a scrapbook of music, cinema, folksy slang, and literature—the classic lyrical key of Dylan's vernacular.

Brash, archetypal DJ Wolfman Jack is "speaking in tongues," spinning a Greek chorus of references and highlights, from Claude Rains's *The Invisible Man* (or Ralph Ellison's *Invisible Man*) to the Book of Revelation's Judgment Day. Dylan name-checks Billy Joel, Stevie Nicks, and the Eagles, asking "where is the truth" alongside the Allman Brothers' Dickey Betts. All is shadow, but also the ear candy of FM radio rises for Shakespearean repetition and emphasis, classic rock and jazz in conversation with the classics. He's a historian, a popular musical Suetonius of tales of the infamous picnic disaster on Bear Mountain in a talking blues, calling out that name or recalling the generals who cleared the way for Elvis and MLK in "Mother of Muses," on the same album as "Murder Most Foul."

More than all else, "Murder Most Foul" is a song about music and musicians. These are the singer's friends and comrades, perhaps the only voices to which Dylan is willing to listen in the same spiritual space of insanity, inaction, and resolve that cannot fill the void of the loss of the father nor the sense of responsibility this foists upon the child. But the songs and singers are like the traditional Jewish prayer for the dead, Kaddish, or traditional wailers at a funeral—yes, Bob Marley undoubtedly plays a prophetic role in popular culture too. These are the voices of consolation.

Even if his vision is dark, Dylan doesn't quite see things as totally dark, at least not yet. The darkness in the color of the blues and the hues could be headed in either direction really, just like the light in that parlor. In "Blind Willie McTell," songs as beautiful as any ever known are still sung, and he witnesses them even if he cannot quite voice them himself. In "Roll on John," his ode to Lennon more than three decades after his murder, Lennon *does* roll on. The Beatles are even cited just after the description of JFK's last breath, coming to hold the children's hand because, well, they want to hold your hand. And in "Murder Most Foul," musicians from Charlie Parker to Patsy Cline as well as citations of titles and lyrics of seventy songs still make beautiful music together, whether they are sinners or saints, or live or dead. The music lives on.

The total of seventy songs cited in "Murder Most Foul" may reference a number from late antiquity; that the Hebrew Bible was translated by the Greeks into seventy languages, the Septuagint; or that Jewish mystics claim the Torah itself speaks in seventy different voices with each utterance. Music is the cultural tissue that keeps a nation's bones from falling apart, and there is no daylight between unknowing, knowing, hearing, truth, and murder most foul. The plays on words are thick and associative. It's a riddle of listening—of observance, of play and distraction—that is not meant be solved or settled, only heard in Dante's loops of colorful stasis.

Here again is the key to Dylan's remembered map of America. It's a musical key, too big to resolve and always witnessed. America *is* its music. An original sin travels from the Civil War to JFK and back in "Murder Most Foul," and all that's left are the voices. But they also seem to provide enough comfort for the singer to survive. "Play," Dylan says in line after line, like the call of Homer in the first line of *The Odyssey*, "Sing, O muse." It's an exhortation to himself and to his listeners. You don't need an actual map to know where America is headed any more than you need a weatherman to know which way the wind blows. But you do need to play.

At a nadir of America's falling into the grip of an invisible virus and waking up to ripped-open wounds more than one hundred fifty years after the Civil War, there is still nothing lower than those slave ships and the murder—murder after murder after murder—of prophetic leaders and plain old people who dreamed of a better place. Don't all come to look for America anymore, Dylan says. Just remember it. Re-member it. Put it back together. And the only way to remember

America is to close your eyes and listen to its song. These songs are also what might still hold it together. Maybe.

Going Back to Brownsville

With an estimated sixteen homes all over the world—a few farms, a houseboat or two, a castle in Scotland, and the mansion in Malibu, as well as a tour bus with a few motorcycles hitched to the back that rarely remains in the same city more than a night or two when he tours—one can safely assume that Bob Dylan, sacred geometrician that he is, is not referring to real estate when he talks about finding his home at the conclusion of Scorsese's *No Direction Home*. He's still the seeker, still restless, not the rock-star aristocrat tending a garden in the British countryside or Connecticut. He is referring to a spiritual home, a place of oneness with his perceived creator, nothing less than a return to the singularity and wholeness that precedes being. That is home, sweet home.

In this context, it's no wonder that Bob Dylan chose *The Odyssey*, the Western canon's most famous coming-home story, as one of the three literary works cited as primary influences in his Nobel lecture. The story of a wounded traveler on the road is embedded in the rock and roll tradition, as it is one of our most known embodiments of the monomyth, an archetype of the seeker—be it of knowledge, love, or a homeland—who must search for something elusive, earthy, and ethereal, no matter the cost.

Ultimately, home is both a place and a metaphor—a home in this world with a partner or family in a neighborhood where life is lived with soulfulness and satisfaction, and also a form of *unio mystica*, a state of melding back into singularity with divinity.

Seekers have no choice but to take on a quest for a spiritual, redemptive home. It's true of Muhammad and Jesus, the children of Israel in the desert, *The Canterbury Tales* and *Don Quixote*, or *On the Road*. For the hero on a quest, the journey is both physical and metaphysical, and it requires the uncomfortable breaking with the comfort of one's original home. "A lot of people can't stand touring," Dylan has said, "but to me it's like breathing. I do it because I'm driven to do it."

Dylan lives (or at least presents) the life of an epic wanderer, sui generis, like the figures in some of his finest songs. In "Brownsville Girl," initially known as "Danville Girl" and one of my favorites, he composed a whopper of a tale with Sam Shepard. Dylan sings,

There was a movie I seen one time, I think I sat through it twice
I don't remember who I was or where I was bound
All I remember about it was it starred Gregory Peck

Like the repetition of a favorite character such as Gregory Peck in a story that mixes itself with the classics that preceded it, plotlines of heroes always feel a bit familiar. They blur together. Also in "Brownsville Girl," Dylan says, "Oh if there's an original thought out there, I could use it right now." Repetition is key to mythic stories, comforting in their predictability, just like coming home. Repeating a familiar plotline with color and flair and their own unique narrative thrills and skills is how a teller of tales makes a tale special. The original thought out there is the teller's charismatic twist on the distinctly unoriginal plotline, that monomyth again.

Way back in Chapter 1, "Salvation," I offered an (un)original thought out there that behind all of Bob Dylan's creative vision—as he said to Nat Hentoff jestingly-seriously in the 1960s and Todd Haynes riffed upon in *I'm Not There*—is seeking salvation. Healing the unforgiving, unforgiven wound of the Civil War, national salvation means coming home because it serves to make America a home for everyone.

Universal and personal concerns can merge, and this is the essence of a contemporary salvational myth, what Campbell called a "public dream." And there's more. An artist lives in some way in the characters they create in the same way that an echo of Dylan's life must resonate in the echoes of his myths. Dylan plays out a salvational epic for self and country to find a way back home from the collective trauma of an endless civil war. It's an American personal, mythical salvation, but it's also a story of the strange path home for Dylan creating himself in all his multitudes.

Maybe this is not the original thought that you and I need right now, but this is the setup as we round third and head for home—that bringing it all back home spiritually is the mythic, political, personal, salvational narrative that defines Bob Dylan's story, the American story, and the divine story as well.

Going back to Brownsville, think of John Brown and his quixotic quest to upend slavery at Harpers Ferry. That there could be a Brownsville would mean a place of Black and white together, not a Monopoly color-coded town, but a town of balance, of equals, that lived up to the ideals America likes to tell others about. There is in that town a home on the range, which means land, of course, but not forty acres and a mule. There's a range of emotion there too, room enough for someone to say how does it feel—or how *did* it feel—to be on their own. *How did it feel to be owned?* America must ask. And then it must listen to the answer.

Never a discouraging word? Is that the range we are talking about? Of course not. If you can't share a discouraging word with your neighbor, if all you can do is talk about the weather, how can you call that feeling at home? Home is where the heart is, but where is the heart of the home, particularly if we are speaking about a nation that has martyred itself in a mythic loop of racial violence time and time again?

Everybody Must Get Homed

In 1966, as he was facing taunts of "Judas" (which we will hear up close in the next chapter) and writing epics of spiritual insight laced with disdain for the world as it was, Dylan rejected every suggestion that he was some kind of messianic figure, some kind of prophet. Maybe he had found the magical redemption of salvation on the jukebox and radio, but it was his and the band's business what they wanted to do with it.

All through the journey ever since—the religious and family trips, the changes in style, the masterworks and dismantling of masterful songs—Dylan kept walking the same pathways, testing the same footprints, embodying the same monomyth. Along the way, something did change. Maybe it was age or spiritual insight, or maybe it was a combination of repetition and a touch of good luck. But the change was a slight shift in the tenor and message of songs that *Rough and Rowdy Ways* affirms in the precise opposite of its title. The same could be said of his return to performing in the recorded concert *Shadow Kingdom* after COVID-19 had pushed musicians off stages everywhere for what seemed like forever. This work was not rough, nor was it rowdy. It was tender, kind, reflective, and, above all else, empathetic.

Dylan, who turned eighty on May 24, 2021, offers the spiritual wisdom that years of rough and rowdy racism, political narcissism, lack of neighborliness, empty platitudes, and manifest tomfoolery drained from the homeland. What's the one missing link all these lazy ways have in common? Empathy. Only a person without empathy can hold a slave or judge another person for the color of their skin. Only a person without empathy can offer a home and then take it away, poison its water, choke its air, pockmark its streets, just to make more mammon to build a bigger mansion in the darkness on the edge of town.

What Dylan demanded from the stage when he was called Judas was for all those jeering or judging or wanting more from him to think for a moment: How does it feel? How does it feel to know what I know when I know it? How does it feel to be who I am, or who I want to be?

No one was ready to answer that question then, but fifty years later, maybe we can.

It's a question that combines humility, confidence, faith, and acceptance as a kind of highest way of being a human, and so does the answer.

If you can feel, or at least try to feel, how the person next to you or singing to you feels, you just may have garnered enough of a fleeting sense of being part of something greater than your own isolated world to understand what the lessons of the righteous sages and prophets and shamans and seers of millennia have taught in every tradition. This is the direction to turn toward when you're on your own and feeling like a complete unknown. And this is what needs to be known. If that question comes to be manifest in the openness of the range, in those wide-open spaces, and migrates toward a hard-won answer of sharing land and myth with generosity and honor, this might be the beginning of turning in the direction of the most important journey of any person, nation, singer, or song—and it is definitely not a direction to travel alone. It's called empathy. It's called service, even holy service. This is the answer blowing in the wind that Dylan's America is missing: empathy. This is the direction home. This is the reconciliation. This is the salvation.

Law

8. Law

They say sing while you slave and I just get bored

It's hard to be a renter on Penny's farm
—"Down on Penny's Farm," the Bentley Boys (1929)

I ain't gonna work on Maggie's farm no more
—"Maggie's Farm," Bob Dylan (1965)

A farm. Agriculture. Cultivation. Culture.

Culture is the art of tending to and elevating shared expression in the pathways of life, the vineyard of voices we nurture, the fruit of societies' labors, the sweet wine that cures with time to mark the connections and experiences of being alive. But for culture to produce these fruits, we need to set boundaries to manage it. There are rules for seeding and growing culture. That's what farms are for.

Down on Maggie's farm, where we pray for rain and sing while we slave, there are powerful cults of culture-making and control, rituals and routines to manage otherwise unrestrained landscapes. Law conquers nature to provide sustenance, but that doesn't mean that it's easy down on the farm. Managing nature in the world at large is challenging, but human nature is even harder to control. North Carolina's Bentley Boys knew it in 1929, and so did Bob Dylan in 1965.

"It's hard to be a renter on Penny's farm. It's a hard time in the country down on Penny's farm," sang the Bentley Boys. Carrying a tune about tenant farmers' facing their greedy landlord Mr. Penny, these Bentleys—of whom there is not a trace beyond this recording—were a world away from the contemporaneous, fancy-pants Bentley Boys on the other side of the Atlantic. That upper-crust crew drove the world's most expensive cars across the same English countryside where the root of the song "Penny's Farm" had probably grown two or three hundred years before. Both groups of boys were fiddling around unaware that the Great Depression was about to turn the world on its head—one crew grasping with callused hands at a whole lot of nothing, the other holding the keys to status and ignition between the fingers of thin leather gloves.

Well on his way to having established his own independence from the typical farmer or factory worker himself in 1965, Bob Dylan sang, "I ain't gonna work on Maggie's farm no more." This was a little less than forty years after "Penny's Farm," a period that included a worldwide economic collapse, the dust bowl migrations, the Holocaust and a world war, the beginning of the Cold War, McCarthy's culture wars, and the beginning of the war in Vietnam.

I jumped from Romantic poet Walt Whitman to the Jazz Age and Robert Johnson in mapping a bit of American culture in the world before rock and roll in chapter 2. Those two seemingly different worlds actually bleed into each other culturally. It's just about the same generation gap between these two farms—Penny's and Maggie's, a world apart in time but still connected by cultural inventory.

Dylan absorbed voices of rural and small-town America firsthand. The country he came from, of course, is called the Midwest, and his portion in the Iron Range was a feeder for heartland heavy metal. He knew wide-open spaces, big skies, hard labor of the hands, close-knit community, and the dominating flow of the weather. He also harvested with care those small-town American tropes, and the music of rural America.

The feel and structure of traditional narratives informed his writing at every turn. Maybe Dylan grabbed seeds or shoots directly from the form and message of the Bentley Boys for a new audience in a new world, squeezing Maggie from a Penny. After all, "Penny's Farm" is included in Harry Smith's *Anthology of American Folk Music*, which seems to have served as an essential cultural record for the folk movement. The musical style and phrasing of "Penny's Farm" is a little sly, kind of funny, but it's not a song of liberation. It's more of a sad complaint.

"Maggie's Farm," however, brings it all back home, getting the young singer's face right up into the mess down there on the farm. This is a manifesto, no holds barred. Whatever farm you're working on, whatever plow you're leaning into, whatever line you're in, if you want to see where things are really at—so says the narrator of "Maggie's Farm"—get up and out of the hole you're in and follow an angry young man wherever disruption leads:

No, I ain't gonna work on Maggie's farm no more
Well, I wake up in the morning
Fold my hands and pray for rain
I got a head full of ideas
That are drivin' me insane
It's a shame the way she makes me scrub the floor

One song calls for resignation, the other for revolution, but both of them stand before man and God and law, pointing a finger at the way things are done in both kinds of nature, human or otherwise. Power and luck, have and have-not, freedom and bondage—Dylan and the brothers meet on the wrong side of the law even if they are on the right side of history.

Bringing this book toward its conclusion, I have talked quite a bit about Bob Dylan framing a mandate for musical salvation that repurposes of the ancient art of memory and a mapping of America as landscapes for holding faith. Now we turn to the third part of the triad that has been accompanying this book since page one: our "man" Dylan and God need to get fully grounded in a structure for spiritual wisdom. This means making it legal. But what are the laws in which we entangle ourselves so that our external and internal natures make sense? Who do we serve, and what purpose does this service and worship fulfill?

In "Absolutely Sweet Marie" from *Blonde on Blonde*, Dylan says that "to live outside the law, you must be honest." It is this balance, and the creed of an outlaw (yes, he's outside of the law), that serves as a template for how to live. If we are meant to be honest outside of the law in order to do what's right, when does living inside the law also affirm truth? What about those hard times in the country when living neither outside nor inside of the law suffices? In thinking about these age-old questions, recall Bob Dylan's responding to a poet mentor in a golf cart in the scene from the film *I'm Not There* I have turned to often: "What does that even mean, man?" Dylan says.

A man from the country, from the highlands, from the Iron Range, Bob Dylan gets his hands dirty on the farm and before the law just like everybody else. He gets mixed up and confused by the ways that law entangles us just as much as it sets straight lines to follow. A married man and a divorced man. A white man and a father. A voter. An agitator. A Christian. A Jew. A record company man. A man of wealth and privilege and many masks. All these roles require knowledge, resolve, trial, and error. Dylan's songs report on the journey of how all these efforts play out, there and back again, inside and out. Here we are at long last: deep in the mud of Maggie's farm with man and God—and law.

What Does That Even Mean, Man?

In the weave of a sacred text—recalling that "*textus*" means a web or something woven in Latin—threads often lead beyond the creator's (and some would say the Creator's) creation. Seeking spiritual wisdom is a kind of archaeology, digging into the layers of words and associations that fortify how a great text pulls many lines of culture and knowledge into its shape. Our greatest texts draw together lines emanating from worlds far beyond themselves.

This memorial phenomenon of sacred text spawning continual elaboration drives the composition of the New Testament, which reframes and expounds upon the Old Testament to shape the Gospels. Exegesis, or the interpretation of scripture, doesn't just provide a fresh twist or deeper understanding about what it inherits. It can create an entirely new system of thought and belief from the text that preceded it. Texts formed out of aggressive commentaries can even put a source text out of business for the new audience of believers the new text serves. This is true for holy sites as well. A temple, a burial ground, or a sacred river is usurped, renamed, and sanctified by the power that conquers it, erasing by sheer creative force an enchanted past in order to inspire a sometimes-dubious future.

The works of a great creator are a timeless dialogue with other worlds of texts and ideas, an ongoing internal dialogue within that artist's own canon, and a springboard for someone out there in the audience or in the stacks to scoop up that basket of meaning and take it even further—or somewhere else altogether.

Exegesis and interpretation release power imbedded in art. For a song like "Desolation Row," a cultural dialogue requiring interpretation and realignment is made explicit. Einstein, the Good Samaritan, and many more get tangled up in the blues of a single mosaic to rework the rules of time itself so that the observer of all these figures can cultivate them into a new world order that makes more sense. The cover montage of *Sgt. Pepper's Lonely Hearts Club Band*, with Carl Jung, Marilyn Monroe, W. C. Fields, and the Beatles, both living and dead posed in a mock-up of a new reality demanding reflection just like a gathering of heroes and gods from any epic, urges forth questions about what that particular mythic crossroads might mean.

In thinking about the entirety of Dylan's work thematically, and assuming that there is something sacred within these songs, I take a similar tack. The songs are talking to each other, old and new, performed and recorded, big impactful hits and throwaways that emerge later to offer something profound.

That is why I am not addressing Dylan's songs in chronological order, but thematically. With all its fits and starts, Dylan's canon is an expansive weaving of musical threads revealing patterns and dialogues within itself and beyond itself. It's like a classical symposium where the toga set would gather around a table to eat, drink, recline, and debate a set of questions concerning a singular topic for hours on end. Dylan may claim to sing while he slaves like a modern-day Simonides, but his platform is also a lively debate on essential ideas, about sixty years' worth, until he's spoken *his* piece on all the pieces and ideas he puts in their new place.

Some of the patterns we find in this dialogue may be intended. A certain phrase or theme is tilled for meaningful effect. Themes of law are a good example of this. Sometimes the raw material with which Dylan works is so rich and his composition is so attuned and playful that unintended associations and meanings take shape as well. Add to the inherent need for thoughtful reflection about any work of this level the fact that Bob Dylan does not like to do anything twice. He probes the same ideas over and over, but from changing perspectives, trying on a new character here, a new voice there. He changes a scene, a lyric, a tempo, or a melody of songs he has already composed. His creative process depends on a permanent state of restless reinvention of his own inventory, even the most familiar song or phrase. Some find this frustrating. Dylan seems to *have to* work this way.

Parsing Dylan's songs as contemporary sacred texts, I incorporate techniques that have been used on such canons for a very long time. Hermeneutics, or exegesis of the word, has roots in the world of Aristotle and Plato, if not earlier. It seems that as long as we have had texts, seekers have wanted to enhance their meaning—from the Greek epics to the Bible to *Hamlet* to the annals of Harry Potter. "What does that even mean, man?" is the question that animates all the techniques of exegetical inquiry.

Sometimes a cigar is just a cigar, a farm is just a farm, and a line is saying what we think it says. But we might also be obligated to ask how a composition is imbedded with moral implications, or try to go further (avoiding Dylan's garbage, please, all you Dylanologists out there) to unpack an allegory or analogy that explains something less demanding attention might not reveal.

Every theme I explore in this book, in fact, is an exegetical framework for gleaning richer meaning than what simple enjoyment of singular or "simple" meanings can bring. Who is this Maggie? What does she symbolize? And are there other ways that Maggie—as a woman, a mother, a lover, an owner, a pawn, or an aspect of the divine—is woven through Dylan's songs? When he says "farm" or addresses the theme of work or slavery, what other layers of wisdom can we glean? Where can this text take us? What is it this text wants?

What Does This Text Even Mean, Man?

Such inquiries of sacred or central texts are common to every tradition. Midrash, for example, is the ancient Jewish art of late antiquity that applies Greek literary explication to the Bible. Then it branches off into the tools that Christianity and Islam use to build spirals of interpretive traditions out of what each religion's prophetic voices reveals within and beyond foundational texts. *What would Jesus do?* is not just a bumper sticker or a T-shirt slogan. It's the question early Christianity called out to the texts it inherited from Judaism, and then it proceeded to create laws in its answers that generated another two thousand years of ongoing sacred dialogue.

In ancient Hebrew, the word "midrash" is derived from a root associated with a person's inquiry or demand of the divine, kind of like a question for an oracle. For the Jewish culture of the late Roman Empire in which Christianity was emerging, the most profound intersection between human and divine identity and experience was embedded in words. After all, according to both Christianity and Judaism, words had created the world itself in the Book of Genesis. In this context midrash came to mean a demand or inquiry not in the sense of going to an aged sage sitting on a hill outside of an oracle, but in the written words passed down from generation to generation from their original reception by Moses in a little hilltop village called Mount Sinai. *What does this text even mean, man?* the midrash asks.

And there's more—there's always more—because midrash, like all hermeneutics of sacred texts, is a two-way exegetical street. "Ask not only what you can do for the text," the midrashic system teaches. "Ask what that text can do for you." Be prepared for the text to ask you questions, to challenge you. And these are often not easy yes-or-no questions either. They are the kinds of questions that happen to animate popular music as well: *Who are you? How does it feel? How long must we sing this song? When will I be loved?* Midrash wants us to ask any question we can imagine within the landscape of a dialogue instigated by a sacred text. It also wants us to be ready to answer whatever questions that sacred text brings up about us.

Sacred texts challenge us to think deeply about how we want to live as we probe them, upping the ante the more those texts mean to us or the tradition in which we live. For those who hold music deep in their hearts, where sacred thoughts and questions are formed, listening to music means being in a dialogue with an oracle. Remember those names—the Doors, the Miracles, Destiny's Child. They're like contemporary caretakers at Delphi facilitating an intimate sacred conversation. We imbed our feelings into the laws these songs lay down.

Yes, music has much to do with simple things. It does not necessarily require gravitas to know who wrote the book of love, though this might explain a lot of things. Music is also one of the most elastic and durable means of conveying lifestyle in the mode of fashion, ways of talking and moving, being cool, which friends are in or out, and opinions about whatever is on a particular song's mind. Music as the stylistic expression of living can be simply beautiful or just plain fun. But it is also a statement of faith. What is your creed? What makes you tick? What do you want? How do you want to live in the world? What is your code?

These are the fundamental issues that Law with a capital "L" is meant to address as well. These are also the questions that animate rock and roll and popular music, just as they animate the Bible or a symposium all-nighter, spilling goblets and souls until they are empty from trying to answer the question, which very often does come down to wanting to know how to love and how to live. Just like the Ten Commandments, just like all the servants trying to make sense of what Maggie's ma is saying about man and God and law, these texts guide us in reflection upon our theological blues, animating our laws and longings.

The Code of the West

There are so many kinds of laws: Religious laws cover everything from diet and sex to who gets to talk with God. There is civil law. Tax law. Criminal law. And then there's the law of Johnny Cash, which his producer and companion Rick Rubin witnessed for himself when Cash began to offer him communion—actual communion with the wafer and the wine and the re-embodiment of a bodily miracle—for years of their friendship, even continuing (according to Rubin) after Cash's death.

Johnny Cash took the law into his own hands. He made his own communion, his own code. And that's a good place to begin thinking about Dylan and the law. Dylan describes his obsession with individualists, both as symbolic figures and specifically as musicians.

"The stuff that trained me to do what I do," Dylan said in 2006, "that was all *individually* based." He continued on the theme:

> That was what you heard—the individual crying in the wilderness...Who's the last individual performer that you can think of?...I'm talking about artists with the willpower not to conform to anybody's reality but their own...It's a lost art form. I don't know who else does it besides myself to tell you the truth.[43]

Even if his description of being the last great American individual still standing goes a little over the top, he is describing a core element of character essential for facing up to the law. Johnny Cash qualifies, leading by example.

Cash was the Man in Black who decided that he would assume the powers of a priest even if this was not the black that any official church had ever granted him. And then, by the power vested in him by the state of being Johnny Cash, a priest he was. Cash symbolically dashed the hierarchy that claims that only certain individuals affirmed by the powers that be can assist someone on the tightrope crossing the peaks of the human-divine divide. But he also affirmed that a certain holiness or grace conveyed by a master to a student is iconoclastically democratic for anyone determined enough to enter this intimate realm.

The fearlessness of a loving tough guy who can offer the bird to maximum lawmen, like Johnny Cash did in his famous photo from San Quentin prison, *and* grant the tender mercies of communion to a friend is a classic typology of a particular kind of hero who doesn't need permission to live the way he knows he must live. This is the outlaw with a superior moral code he uses to outflank the corruption and boredom of the pedestrian world. Breaking out of the status quo, the outlaw accesses life in ways people on Main Street can only dream of knowing.

As much as with martyrs, Dylan's work holds a fascination with outlaws, especially those of the American West. The archetypes of the rock star and the new sheriff in town go well together. Think of *Double Elvis*, Andy Warhol's silkscreen of the King drawing a gun in a shootout. This is a piece of art that Warhol gave to Dylan (some say Dylan just took it) as part of an awkward showdown at high noon at the Factory when the two seemed to have the spurs on their boots to kick ahead the cultural zeitgeist wherever they wanted it to go in the mid-1960s. Legend has it that Dylan—after finishing off the few minutes of a fidgety screen test—threw Elvis into the back of his car like a hipster Jesse James and sped away. He says he traded that image of Elvis for a couch sometime later.

Think of Bad Company, the Eagles, or Bon Jovi sporting cowboy kitsch and weaving their own version of an outlaw narrative into their songs. Think of Gram Parsons and Nudie suits. But none other than Johnny Cash warns not to make too much of Wild West mythologies. In "Drive On," a song from one of the albums of Cash's twilight years produced by Rick Rubin, Cash's narrator communes with the spirit of a fallen friend in Vietnam, remembering the long walk in the jungle in the rain where he died. No one in his posse had wanted anything to do with the poses of John Wayne in the moments before the unit was ambushed. They were just scared. As Cash's surviving soldier keeps moving through life, becoming a trucker, driving to find some dignity and order while protecting himself and his family, he gets choked up over the memory of the dead soldier who haunts him.

It's not just Rambos and MAGAs who choke themselves—and choke others—with the cowboy myth. If you were a Native American, a woman, a person of color, or another "other" outside of the cowboy class and code, the default position of cowboy culture was violence, not morality. But lurking in reception of these good, bad, and ugly outlaws is a statement from Bob Dylan I've already mentioned, a creed.

As Dylan sings in "Absolutely Sweet Marie," to be an outlaw, to be *outside the law*, a person needs to have rules. This is what it means to be honest. Honesty provides a moral compass and moral code. To draw outside of the lines of the law, you had better be someone we can trust, who knows their stuff, because all you are is your name—even if you have made that name up, like outlaws from Bob Dylan to Billy the Kid—and your word. And, like the lead character in "John Wesley Harding," you had better never make a foolish move. On that same eponymous record, Dylan sings in "I Am a Lonesome Hobo": "Stay free from petty jealousies, live by no man's code, and hold your judgment for yourself lest you wind up on this road." A true outlaw code is completely sui generis. It belongs to no one *but* the outlaw.

Dylan did not invent this creed any more than Johnny Cash invented communion, but Dylan, like Cash with the wine and the wafer, makes an inherited tradition of the law his own. There is indeed something called the Code of the West. It's a phrase—"Code of the West"—sometimes twinned with the novel of the same name by Zane Grey, famous for his many Western novels and short stories. Dylan may have read some of them as a child, including Grey's most famous book, 1912's *Riders of the Purple Sage*—not to be confused with the *New* Riders of the Purple Sage, a hippie cowboy band that Dylan's friend Jerry Garcia and other members of the Grateful Dead joined from time to time. If he didn't read the books, Dylan probably saw his share of the more than one hundred films adapted from Zane Grey's fiction.

This was not the first time that men on horses taught a mixed bag of social lessons about how to live in the world according to a code of honor. King Arthur's Knights of the Round Table provided a colorful set of mythic narratives to inculcate society with the values of chivalry through horse-ridin', tail-kickin', yes-ma'amin' men in the field. And chivalry had its share of grace and goodness concerning honor, civility, and piety despite its inherent and Middle Ages-appropriate male dominance. It's one thing to tell people to be honorable and do the right thing. It's something else to model doing the right thing through colorful characters facing real or imagined moral challenges.

That does not mean that Johnny Cash's soldier of honor in "Drive On," who faced, as he says, a smiling tiger of death in the jungles of Vietnam, can get his friend back, or that ol' Waylon Jennings, Cash's latter-day touring companion in the Highwaymen with Kris Kristofferson and Willie Nelson, can bring Buddy Holly back after giving up his seat on a puddle jumper airplane to save his friend from another freezing bus ride. The plane went down, Jennings lived instead of dying, Dylan was convinced that Holly stared communion into his young eyes from the stage three days prior, and then came the wreck of "American Pie."

Doing the right thing according to the code may or may not mean surviving, let alone producing any other tangible form of reward. You may slay the dragon. You may lose an arm, or even your life. The code is an organizing principle for a moral universe when the rules of the farm are too restrictive or corrupt. But no one gets a free ride. Freedom to be free from the laws of the status quo inevitably requires its burdens too.

Pawn Town

An outlaw's noble go-it-aloneness signals danger on both sides of the choice to be an outsider. First, there's the danger of having to pay whatever price is required when an outsider's path inevitably leads to conflict. People are troubled by difference, especially when it challenges people in power, and it can get lonely going against the grain. Releasing oneself from society's laws induces new debts. You might lose your lover to someone more aligned with the system by defending a higher honor, like John Wayne's Tom Doniphon in *The Man Who Shot Liberty Valance*. But this acceptance of danger is also a response to something broken in the law, something even more dangerous and corrupt than what the outlaw faces *outside* of it. Staying within the law can be ten times worse.

I have already mentioned Greil Marcus's juxtaposition of Dylan's exilic basement songwriting and the "secret history" of the American republic, an imagined assemblage of characters and customs aligned in an unspoken code for navigating the shadow side of human and nature's nature. We can imagine another iteration of natural law emergent too. It's a farm gone to seed, overgrown, undernourished, and left to its own devices. This is a world dipping in and out of chaos, "Scarlet Town," a netherworld from Dylan's 2012 album *Tempest*.

The narrator claims to have been born there, but it's a home he's cast out of as well. Looking back on his home, the chaos he describes in "Scarlet Town" reflects a slippery slope leading to the unformed and void days before words in the Book of Genesis gave shape to the very first farm, the Garden of Eden. And the place is falling apart, a decaying shell of a good old-fashioned, law-abiding, law-and-order town:

In Scarlet Town, the end is near
The seven wonders of the world are here
The evil and the good living side by side
All human forms seem glorified

Put your heart on a platter and see who'll bite
See who'll hold you and kiss you good night
There's walnut groves and maple wood
In Scarlet Town crying won't do you no good

In Scarlet Town, all opposites and archetypes cancel out. It is every person and their uncontrolled passions for themselves. Order breaks down. Chaos reigns. Of course, this is not unfamiliar territory for Dylan. "I accept chaos," he once said. "I wonder if chaos accepts me."

Like Marcus's Kill Devil Hills or Riddle, Minnesota, the unraveling nexus Todd Haynes manifested for Richard Gere as Dylan, watching a funereal Gabriel's horn rendition of "Going to Acapulco" in the film *I'm Not There*, there are no pranks in Scarlet Town, no humor, because everything seems to be a cruel joke. A dead girl in a coffin draws forward this particular scene of *I'm Not There*, her face painted white like Dylan's during the Rolling Thunder Revue tour. It's a reference to one of the murder ballads collected by Harry Smith and imbibed by Dylan, this form of haunting tale serving as a common, jarring witnessing in musical folkways for the ultimate violence against women.

Like the generation before the flood, from whom Noah and his family were plucked to start the world all over again, Haynes depicts Dylan's many musical requiems for entire communities that cannot find social equilibrium, let alone safety, inside or outside of the law.

Before the Flood happens to be the name of the live album Dylan and the Band released after their 1974 tour, Dylan's first in eight years. This is a powerful biblical allusion. It's said that Noah was the only righteous person of his generation. All living things but for Noah and his immediate family and the animals they gathered were flooded out of existence. Noah was saved, according to the Hebrew Bible, because he lived by the divine laws that governed life after the harmony of the Garden of Eden was disrupted by a snake slithering up to Eve near the

Tree of Knowledge and Cain and Abel's conflict marking the world's first murder.

"[T]he earth was filled with lawlessness," says Genesis 6:11. Like other biblical times of lawlessness during the Tower of Babel or the books of Joshua, Judges, and Ruth, life before the flood—*Before the Flood*, that is—was such an antithesis of civilization that it was completely destroyed. "Scarlet Town" offers a similar sense of a Code of the West corrupted to its core. It is a song of a chaotic mythic past and future—like people in Florida living in abandoned motels without electricity and plumbing outside of Disney World because of COVID-19. It is a ringless, ringleaderless circus. Seams of the fabric of what makes up a town are torn. Cultures of sacred routine and tradition turned to cults of QAnon, projecting the worst of murder ballads and cheap perversions of science fiction paranoia upon made-up enemies.

Weeds grow back through the cracks of towns living in such illusions, and they grow back scarlet. Like blood. Like the letter. Like Scarlett O'Hara in the paean to the Old South known as *Gone with the Wind*, where in the end no one gives a darn. Published by Margaret Mitchell just seven years after the Bentley Boys sang on the farm, twenty-nine years before Maggie heard about the troubles, and twenty-seven before the going, going, gone with the wind of "Blowin' in the Wind," *Gone with the Wind* affirms a softer side of the KKK-ogling *Birth of a Nation*, America's cross-eyed obsession with the Civil War as a romantic myth everyone could love—but for the millions of ancestors and allies it erased.

Scarlet Town doesn't come out of nowhere. It's not some here-today, gone-with-the-wind-tomorrow operation. It's not one of those fake Western towns, thrown-up façades supported by two-by-fours somewhere in the desert that only last long enough for the day's shoot of a spaghetti Western. It's got a Main Street and a barbershop just like everywhere else. Like the site of a murder ballad, or one of the songs about a demon lover Harry Smith also collected, it started as Every Town, USA, a city, a farm, a community that somehow got off track.

Before the flood, someone had put a shoulder to the plow to make the farms, to build the buildings, to cultivate the culture according to the law before it all went to pot, but whatever glue of morality or neighborliness held the town together melted away once shared purpose got lost. Back in the day, people had the capacity to work together for great things, like the generation after the flood that built the Tower of Babel, which reached like the Twin Towers to the heavens, just after Noah's ark saved a remnant of those who had come before them.

We visited some of those working people in the hardscrabble Bentley Boys' struggling under the boot of a landowner, real-life versions of the "poor white man" of Dylan's "Only a Pawn in Their Game" (1964). The law may become so corrupt and degrading in any form that from Hattie Carroll to Hollis Brown to "Brownsville Girl" to a woman he knows down in Alabama, it must be destroyed before it destroys us.

Pawn Town might be a better name for a place of such repute. It's a place that emerges somewhere in the mix of the Civil War and (as R.E.M. might say) *Fables of the Reconstruction*, a world a lot like Scarlet Town before the flood or just after it, with everyone—Black and white—working for the ones that run Maggie's farm.

The first thing Noah and his sons did after coming to land and stepping out of the ark was to plant a vineyard—a farm, cultivation, culture—a vessel for finding sustenance while controlling nature. In the next biblical scene, he and his boys got drunk (remember that biblical time is mythic and very unlike our own), after which things went so sour that the drunk sons lingered with seeming sexual intent beside their own father, who had passed out from drinking too much wine. So goes human nature, a force even the best-laid plans and vineyards cannot control.

Pawn Town produces a culture of shadows, a cluster of humanity descended from that cross that Dylan said agricultural, mercantile America was crucified upon from the start: slavery, forced labor, systemic power thriving on poverty, all pitting white against Black. The insightful instigation of "Only a Pawn in Their Game" reframes Jim Crow and anticipates MAGA, "the poor white man" manipulated to hate people of color so that he himself can be oppressed by a waxen white lawmaker, a carpetbagging, shapeshifting con artist. It's a preview of Nixon's Southern Strategy, Dylan singing "Only a Pawn in Their Game" at the March on Washington next to Dr. Martin Luther King Jr. a few years before Nixon invented it as such, having just lost by, or perhaps because of, a whisker to the youthful JFK, who was himself soon to be removed from the White House stage by a murder most foul.

Keeping Up with the Mr. Joneses

Who are the lawmakers who rule Pawn Town with controlled scarcity while wielding the cudgel of race? Who are the nameless and faceless Boys from Brazil who set this cycle of ill repute in motion and monitor its progress? Did they arrange for JFK's assassination, gerrymander maps with Nixon, feed the media racist fantasies about the Central Park Five and Obama's birth certificate with Donald Trump?

Dylan takes on the *Mad Men* leaders in the shadows, the operators in gray pinstriped suits, the smoke-signaling, dog-whistling, smoky-boardroom overlords pushing left and right overboard to extremes from the middle of the road to prop up and keep up with the jones of the Joneses. His "Ballad of a Thin Man" from 1965 is a takedown of the man of the law in five round verses.

"Well, you walk into the room like a camel and then you frown," Dylan sings in the last one. Each verse has brought this man of power and judgment more and more uncomfortably into a scene of societal chaos. We have met the enemy, Dylan says with descriptions of an ominous culture war. We have met the enemy, he says, and they look like someone we know—well dressed, well heeled, and holding court in a nondescript office down the hall:

You put your eyes in your pocket
And your nose on the ground
There ought to be a law
Against you comin' around
You should be made
To wear earphones

Because something is happening here
But you don't know what it is
Do you, Mr. Jones?

Mr. Jones symbolizes civil society's movers and shakers, hindered by his own ignorance and confusion as he governs everyone else with cruelty. Dylan imagines Mr. Jones, a name as common as Main Street, missing out on any chance of understanding what is happening here. There is a law against his coming around, his ears stopped up and marking his isolation.

Often booed and cursed on the stage like an early iteration of the Sex Pistols or the Cramps on the tour with the Band (sans Levon Helm) when they were still the Hawks in 1965–66, maelstrom versions of "Ballad of a Thin Man" and "Like a Rolling Stone," which are readily available in both Dylan's bootleg series and on YouTube, held up poles of purpose, of confrontation and blame. But those poles also held a burden much too heavy to bear.

As is fitting for a rock and roll myth, a concert in Manchester, England, flashed a sudden pivot in the plot as a shout of "Judas!" came from a crowd immersed in the energy emanating from the stage. Fans were upset at Dylan's electrification and laying into the release of passions facilitated by almost any kind of rock and roll, which this most certainly was not. This was fierce rock, rock of liberation from many things, including its audience. "I don't believe you," Dylan snarled, then commanded his band to play the next song as loud as they could. "Once upon a time you dressed so fine…" Dylan continued.

Here comes another fantasy removed from time, once upon a time, and the story once again of an ungrounded, emancipated rolling stone untethered to society. But a glimpse of forever was contained in those moments of conflict, a shift in points of view between artist and audience, their natures, their laws, and the combustible culture they were cultivating together. This and these moments did something to Dylan as a performer, and perhaps, though no one can really know but him, as a person too. It pulled him inward, and as we untangle the law, we will see what this change both traps and sets free.

After the 1966 motorcycle crash on a break from the tour that brought shouts of "Judas!" at Manchester and had been meant to continue for many more dates, everything slowed down. A musical persona of resignation and remove appeared in what would be known as *The Basement Tapes*, which was recorded offhandedly for kicks and as songwriting demos in the year or so that followed. *John Wesley Harding* (December 1967) and *Nashville Skyline* (April 1969) were also born. Tripping along the watchtower, after Mr. Jones seemed to have gotten the upper hand, maybe life *was* but a joke, and the music got acoustic, homey, and laconic as a result.

If "Only a Pawn in Their Game" had faced the present and demanded immediate justice and accountability at the start of his career, "Scarlet Town," released a lifetime or so later in 2012, sees the world as a reflection of dark myths that cannot be changed, only meditated upon, a world eternally both just before and just after the flood as people prove their inherent weakness time and time again. Earthly law, which cannot be changed, means that people *only* make foolish moves despite John Wesley Harding's warning.

No Neutral Ground

"I don't get it. Why would [Dylan] go for Jesus at a late time like this?"

That's what Leonard Cohen was said to have asked Jennifer Warnes when he heard that the Jewish-born Dylan had entered into evangelical Christianity at some point in 1978.

It is one of the great conundrums of rock and roll, how Dylan, the agitating, rule-busting, iconoclastic, fire-breathing prophet, became an agitating, rule-busting, iconoclastic, fire-breathing prophet. Or maybe it's not such a mystery—right?—that a musician steeped in the music and mythology of the Church, a longing witness to a pawned America died on a cross, himself taunted as Judas, would be drawn to try on Christian law in all its power and glory. This is really no surprise at all.

Of all the intangible elements contributing to Bob Dylan's sustaining genius—prodigious recall of the breadth and depth of American song and a restless and creative spirit twinned with abiding intellectual curiosity—none has been more powerful than his ability to confound expectations. Pop vocalists on the radio were not supposed to sing through their noses or sputter and growl from their throats, but Dylan changed that. He unquestionably grabbed and repurposed a range of vocal traditions extant for a very long time, but in pushing that repurposing to the radio and its laws of appropriateness, he put a crack in the mold, if not breaking it altogether.

Not long after establishing himself on the charts, and seemingly overnight for his fans, he swapped lucid, intimate acoustic protest tunes for esoteric, electric epics. Radio songs were supposed to be three minutes long, but Dylan changed that rule, too. The second half of "Like a Rolling Stone" served as its own B-side. Disc jockeys simply flipped the record over halfway through. A pivotal figure in 1960s counterculture, Dylan all but disappeared from public view as the underground coalesced, reaching a symbolic head in 1969 in Woodstock. Then he was a no-show at the music festival named after the place where he lived, even though it was just a car ride through marathon miles of traffic down the road from his house.

In what was for many perhaps the most unusual period of Dylan's career, the late 1970s, Dylan became, to the shock of many of his fans, a born-again Christian. To add what may have seemed like insult to injury for the Rock and Roll Empire, his albums *Slow Train Coming* (1979), *Saved* (1980), and *Shot of Love* (1981) were steeped in Christian imagery and proselytizing intent, anchored by a series of tours with the clear-eyed focus of a missionary aiming to capture as many souls for the good guys as he possibly could muster.

But Dylan's conversion could have been predicted by those paying attention to his canon as well as the chaos around him. By the time a few close confidants in his circle helped him find the Vineyard Christian Fellowship Church, where Dylan studied and prayed, he was a "witness" in the realm of newly fundamentalist Christian acolytes and church veterans who already had formed a minor movement of their own after wide-ranging, cross-movement calls for emancipation in the 1960s and 1970s. The tumult of drugs, social and political burnout, and Mr. Jonesian pushback against liberation left many people broken and tired in ways that meant that evangelical answers about the law, both passionate and binary, made easy spiritual pickings out of vulnerable souls.

Dylan's religious stances over the years betray vulnerability to extremes and a profound sense of drama for which a messianic soft sell works. Exposed to changes enhanced by his innate, dynamic spiritual character and the trials and tribulation of divorce while the demons came to roost for a generation that lived through a wild-goose-seeking emancipation, Dylan plunged headlong into the quest for salvation in the late 1970s. Maybe he showed up at Chabad-Lubavitch Shabbat programs in Brooklyn's Crown Heights a few years later, and at Chabad on both coasts on the High Holy Days ever since, but Dylan's fans still reflect on this Christian period with dismay—and not just because of Dylan's religion.

Most of the time, Dylan embodies a multilayered approach to any subject—especially the law—with wordplay, rich sets of allusions, insinuations, irony, and clusters of unexplained questions smoothing the corners of sharp extremes. With a few exceptions, the so-called Christian period of Dylan's work—while layered, profound, and rich lyrically and musically—is more literal, humorless, and blunt than any of his songwriting before or since.

While the songs and performances of this phase are something of an archipelago in the land of Dylan, one would be hard-pressed to find a precise beginning and end for the influence of Christian theology and longing on his work. It is there because it is in American music so integrally. But this is the period—three, maybe four or five albums depending on how you count—where Dylan's Christian passion is particularly fierce. The law is everywhere, and there is only one that's real. As he sings in "Precious Angel": "Ya either got faith or ya got unbelief and there ain't no neutral ground."

This fiery, inflexible faith was like a dam that would inevitably crack and fail against the tides of myth and purpose that had fed Dylan's mix of faith and unbelief since the beginning. There are clues for how the dam came apart both before and after that dam was constructed, and most important, how its blueprint of faith continued to serve Dylan's imagination long after the rush of mystic, mythic law burst through it. There would be no flood to wash away Dylan's grounding in thinking and writing about the law. He would continue to be observant, as his announcement of "murder most foul" demanded. He would continue to refer to the divine, to martyrs and saviors, to holiness, to sin, to creation and the Creator, but with a subtlety and nuance that demanded a "yes, and…" approach to living inside or outside of the law. Not so in the time of "Precious Angel." In that time, he was as all in religiously as all in could be.

For those who require absolute allegiance to the law or who privilege a fundamentalist approach to the fundamentals of religion, Dylan might have been both before and after his evangelical phases as wanting to have his spiritual cake of law and eat it too. But ironic resignation, respectful believing, and loving doubt are hallmarks of the contemporary spiritual wisdom that Dylan is both a part of and helps shape. It surely plants both faith and unbelief in a passionate, animated, and decidedly *not* neutral ground. But this does not mean there's *not* something deeply spiritual and wise happening down on that neutral ground on that particular farm. In fact, the very opposite is true. It's on the neutral, non-fundamentalist ground that spiritual wisdom is cultivated best today. This makes our period both part of the exception and part of the rule when it comes to the art of renewing the fundamentals of man and God and law.

Another Man from Another Country

Dylan is part of living tradition reflecting on religion. I have reached back five hundred years to seek roots for the Rock and Roll Empire in Martin Luther and the Age of Reason, as well as two thousand years more to think about memory and a whole range of themes that animate the symposium of popular music and culture.

As American music was truly cooking up its unique flavor of blues and jazz and F. Scott Fitzgerald was writing the books that Mr. Jones would later read, Franz Kafka was stirring a literary cauldron of faith and doubt in Prague, sensing the impending doom in ongoing war and strife, critiquing work and religion, ritualizing longing, languishing in mysticism and myth, and giving voice to a spiritual wisdom for modernity that can be heard all over Dylan's work, but particularly at the edges of the period of his most visceral encounter with faith in the form of fundamentalist Christianity.

Dylan has told us a lot about what he reads and when he reads it, and Richard F. Thomas, in *Why Bob Dylan Matters*, has done stellar work tracking Dylan's forays through translations of classical Greek and Latin texts. With regard to Kafka, there seems to be no clear intersection of engagement. Still, if texts are like mirrors their authors put up for the world to see itself, and if the works of Dylan and Kafka were juxtaposed face to face, they would surely linger and stare, enraptured by what they shared.

My favorite reading of Franz Kafka's "Before the Law" is performed by Orson Welles in his 1962 adaptation of Kafka's novella *The Trial*, the full narrative within which the excerpt "Before the Law" appears. As a cultural side note, recall that at the age of twenty-five—exactly the age of Bob Dylan in his most fertile period of creativity and icon busting—Welles saw right through his own Mr. Jones, William Randolph Hearst/ Citizen Kane. That the great Man of the Law Mr. Kane was nothing more than a scared child who had lost his Rosebud remains one of the most insightful moments of critique in popular culture I know.

The name of the man who is made a joke in Kafka's "Before the Law" means everything, but it is not a proper name. He is called "a man from the country." In German the term "*ein Mann vom Lande*" may be a play on the Hebrew phrase "*am ha'aretz*," which means not just "one from the country" but "one without knowledge," an ignorant man, a kind of redneck. In Kafka's tale this man is reduced to becoming a sniveling child "before the law," like Kane remembering his Rosebud or Mr. Jones at a total loss as he walks into a room where "there ought to be a law against [his] comin' around."

Kafka's man from the country appears at a gate behind which lives the law. A gatekeeper jives him a bit, but for the most part, this is a story in which nothing, truly nothing, is really happening here and you know precisely what it is. A quiet question here, a meek protest there; the man from the country cannot will himself to push past the guard and crack open the gate. He waits, he ages, he despairs, he mourns, and he dies there—unenlightened and unfulfilled. And after all of that, when his diminishment is all but complete, the guard scoffs that that gate of mysteries before the law had always been meant just for him—if only he had chosen to open it.

If only…if only Kafka's man from the country had bucked up and followed his instincts, a little law of the jungle, perhaps, he could have broken through to his fullness and emancipation. But he had no instincts, so he waited in line like a good citizen—not a Citizen Kane who owns the line and the guard and the gate and the law. Instead, the man from the country waited for the law to do the right thing and take care of him, just like Rosebud would have done. His life force seeps away. He watches himself become helpless. He cannot take care of himself before the law, and no one takes care of him, so he disappears, not even enough of a self anymore to be a pawn in their game.

Moshe Idel writes in *Kabbalah: New Perspectives*[44]—an explication of Jewish mystical traditions spanning from the time of Jesus to the time of Madonna—that "Before the Law" is a fable for the contemporary decline of mystical knowledge in religious traditions stunted by allowing flat, rational answers to dominate layered questions of spiritual wisdom. From Jewish orthodoxies to Muslim fundamentalism to evangelical Christianity—an echo of both the Enlightenment, which went for science, and Romanticism, which went for feeling—Kafka presages the dilemma that communities are being deprived of the complexity of mystery and enlightenment that religious systems can express. Instead, they often get a humorless gatekeeper and the evaporation of their agency. For Idel, the spiritual paralysis of the "man from the country" is emblematic of an entire generation of disenchanted seekers who have lost the keys to the locked gate of the splendor in the palace of faith that awaits them if they can only think and feel for a moment for themselves.

Kafka's man from the country gets both a kick in the pants and a pat on the back in Dylan's "Señor (Tales of Yankee Power)." It's a striking parallel to "Before the Law" and lands in 1978, with Dylan on the cusp of his evangelical leap of faith. "Señor" is the Spanish term for "lord" and is used to refer to Jesus, the savior, whom Dylan is addressing directly—Jesus the guard whom Dylan asks for advice and succor throughout the song, but also rebel Jesus, wise and iconoclastic Jesus, the Jesus who offers no quarter and takes no gold coin when it comes to corruption of the law. Dylan asks him—from Lincoln County Road (where that old outlaw Billy the Kid made his beans) to Armageddon—is that all there is, Señor?

This song is layered with allusions, awash in color, and unfolds within a melody for the ages—God-honest rock of ages. Then the final verse blows up the law. First comes total alienation. Dylan is a rolling stone and an outlaw. There are at least three choices before him: resignation to his fate, Señor looking on; alienation, walking away from those tables and that possible savior; or, on the third hand, revolution.

Even though he knows the option to blow it all up is his for the taking, he asks Señor for permission to go all the way. He wants not just a fellow traveler, not just a contra, but an authority to bless his resolution for revolution:

Let's overturn the tables
Disconnect these cables
This place don't make sense to me no more
Can you tell me what we're waiting for, Señor?

This question to Señor, or rather, this request, is unanswered. What would Señor do? What would Dylan do? What would Jesus do? The questions sound like the beginning of an answer. Turning the tables. And overturning them. Cutting the cables. Starting over, lawless. But the revolution here is not televised. It's not anything at all. Señor does not answer, a saxophone solo draws out the song, and seemingly, like Kafka's man from the country, even if Dylan's seeker has more zest, he waits outside the gate without liberation and without an answer. Next thing you know, a fundamentalist slow train is coming around the bend.

Biographically at least, a very different likely-unlikely revolution follows, Dylan converting this passion to old-time religion, then hitting the vinyl and the road to tell the world—he himself a Señor for so many—not only that those cables he saw with Señor *can't* be cut, but that they lead only back to Señor. So many questions posed about life and law, faith and unbelief, and for a while at least, the world finally got its answer. For the most part, it was unsatisfied, even annoyed, that rock's artist of salvation had had the gall to take a shot of love for himself.

The Jokerman Was on Me

In 1983, five years after "Señor" was released, here comes the album *Infidels*. Infidels, of course, are outlaws by another name, the ones who reject the holy law of a tradition to go it alone. It's a collection of songs in which Dylan pulls out of the tight connective embrace of the laws of Christianity, trying to put his arms instead around the murmurings of self-doubt. Here is "Jokerman," a curriculum for the legal fragments that an outlaw or a heretic assembles to remake a code of honor that a fundamentalist approach has replaced:

> Well, the Book of Leviticus and Deuteronomy
> The law of the jungle and the sea are your only teachers

As a student of the law, before he strikes out on his own again, he's not leaving everything behind. In fact, from testament to testament or tradition to tradition, he carries a kind of seed for a way of doing and seeing the world that still connects back to law as Law, even as an infidel. He describes, in the most condensed way in which one could summarize it, a legal essence much like what Jesus and Hillel the Elder agreed upon: that after all the ink and blood spilled over dos and don'ts, the Bible can be explained in a single sentence, as mentioned in chapter 4, called the Golden Rule, which states across traditions something like "Do unto others as you would have them do unto you."

First is Leviticus, the book of the Hebrew Bible most aligned with the priestly cult of ancient Israel, the logbook and manual for the operation of the Temple and all its sacrifices and rituals. It is a book about purity, hierarchy, and above all else, the precise measurements of how to bring the divine into interaction with the world. Then comes the Book of Deuteronomy, which means "the repeating," a kind of reprise of all the preceding four books of the Hebrew Bible in condensed form. It's the greatest hits, a Bible for your pocket. Next, Dylan wanders far from the Bible to the Law of the Jungle, which I hear as a world without law, pure nature, no farms, no farmers, just wild and chock-full of danger, a place where no Jokerman should ever really be. And then, finally, there is the sea. Ask any poet, or Herman Melville, about the wisdom that makes humanity seem like less than a grain of sand when living among the ways of the sea, where all the sailors but cast-off Ishmael drown, and the captain goes mad.

Dylan addresses himself, Jokerman, in the third person, as if he himself is a stranger, a visitor to his own life. What a joke. He has learned the ancient laws and still winds up here, laughing at himself or being laughed at. Joni Mitchell famously described a starlet at a Hollywood party as like that old mask of Greek drama, all release, laughing and crying just two ways of calming the same troubled spirit.

This is the painful dichotomy that brings us to a crossroads for Dylan and the law. He has learned society's rules and called them out as a young man. He has tried to run wild and free as well. Trying out many masters, his voice of frustration and irony takes us back to a voice that predates Dylan's by a generation, Kafka's, even as it carries a very similar bundle of conflicts: a self that feels chosen for something unique and profound but is unable to open the gate to its fate and enter it.

Dylan's songs rollick in love with the farm of faith, and his characters are often standing in line, waiting for their number to come up, because that's life. He rejects ignorance, rejects the unexamined or unexplained life, and longs for a place with the divine. With a resignation in "Blind Willie McTell" that "God is in his heaven and we all want what's His, but power and greed and corruptible seed seem to be all that there is," there's another outlet that comes up shining in Dylan's world that might foretell a peaceful middle ground that embraces the fundamentals of faith without fundamentalism's taking away one's soul.

When he goes down into the parlor, resigning himself to life that transcends law or law that plays too rough, he relives his dreams to fine a reprieve. This is "tryin' to get to heaven before they close the door." Again.

Beyond the law, beyond love, even beyond music, there are amorphous dreams, which provide both escape from life as well as the raw material out of which life is formed. One can function in the world, play the games, even dabble in fully embodying oneself in its rules. But there is also a place—call it pure imagination—a place of dreams and disembodiment, where the soul lives unencumbered. Law is an exercise in preparation for letting everything go:

Thinking of a series of dreams
Where the time and the tempo fly
And there's no exit in any direction

'Cept the one that you can't see with your eyes
Wasn't making any great connection
Wasn't falling for any intricate scheme
Nothing that would pass inspection
Just thinking of a series of dreams

For the living, law means schemes and connections, inspections and directions of the soul and others. A disembodied voice in Dylan, a voice adrift, but seemingly happy, comes to question whether full embodiment is even possible living inside the law, while living outside of it gets too lonely. Is real life elsewhere, beyond the body, in the farmless, fieldless, lawless netherworld of raw imagination and spirit?

Pushing open that gate, getting behind the law, and finding out what came before the law, what's behind the gate, there may be a place very much like a series of dreams. To learn and live before the law may be the price one pays to have the courage to finally open the door, close one's eyes, and leave the law for good. Until that time, cultivating faith and unbelief on neutral ground—with fierce passion and moderation, fancy that—may be the wisest spiritual answer.

Can "How does it feel?" be codified? What is the role of hierarchy, intellect, worship, or ritual in defining how best to live? In the end, I don't know where Bob Dylan stands with all of this, but before venturing into what might come after him, I offer Bob Dylan's Ten Commandments to continue the conversation.

The original Decalogue written in the Hebrew Bible in Exodus 20: 2-17 and Deuteronomy 5: 6-21 begins a line marking the beginning of a landscape of faith—"I the LORD am your God"— followed by nine directives, each representing a category of religious practice to be observed by believers. Bob Dylan tends to lead by example and not explain. I can follow that advice, though not to the letter of the law:

1. Something is happening, and I told you what it is
2. Change, while being constant
3. Stay away from pranks
4. Know that God is watching
5. Don't pay attention to what they say
6. Everybody must get stoned
7. Love until you're sick of love, and then love some more
8. Keep moving
9. Read everything
10. Don't follow leaders, follow teachers

It's not clear if this list is teachable or actionable as religious law. To live inside *or* outside the law while being honest means that we cannot ever know with complete certainty what the law wants from us—what is right, what is truth, even what is law.

A life of seeking salvation, lived humbly, empathetically, and faithfully, is a continual attempt to stay as close to the possibility of harmony amongst man and God and law as one can. There are good days and bad days, days of closeness and days of distance. Religious practice does not guarantee perfecting a soul, and it can be a very poor means of soothing the gloom of longing or doubt. But practice means repetition, like Bob Dylan singing his beloved "Tumbling Tumbleweeds" over and over until it becomes something the world did not know before.

Music is never static, nor should spiritual wisdom by stuck in time like the frozen moment of Pompeii. Listening to Dylan over and over, like listening to law or tradition, means gleaning something unexpected and fresh through immersion in what is old. It means staying close enough to traditional questions about man and God and law to allow for the possibility of moments of learning, love, or revelation in which repetition reveals a moment of insight or intimacy, both of the law and beyond it.

9. AD: After Dylan

Ain't no altars on this long and lonesome road

———— ▬ ————

The Rock and Roll Hall of Fame induction ceremony is the holy altar of the Rock and Roll Empire. *Holy, holy, holy are rock's lords and hosts.*

Americans love their halls of fame. These pantheons enshrining achievement first entered the consciousness of the United States at the end of the 19th century, with roots in Europe, and now there is a hall of fame for every flavor and fetish of achievement, great or small. Ranking, progress, determining who are the best practitioners in a particular field, is an American obsession. But neither the science nor the art of choosing what or who is best is necessarily fixed or pleasing, and the choices of who or what is the best cannot outflank the biases that define the fields of endeavor themselves.

Housed in Cleveland, Ohio, built by and for the gods, heroes, and faithful of rock to recognize its rites and tell its tale after the moment for the liberation it had promised to deliver had already passed, the Rock and Roll Hall of Fame—like the Rock and Roll Empire—honors too few women and people of color and not enough artists working at the edges of music. It just doesn't pass the smell test for creators and fans who see it as a hulking distraction from what really matters about music.

There have been induction-ceremony nights of honest-to-goodness rock-star craziness to entertain and amaze those who appreciate such things—like Mike Love of the Beach Boys lambasting the shoddy state of his contemporaries, including Paul McCartney and Mick Jagger, while Bob Dylan shook his head and smiled. There have been ego trips that keep everyone from Guns N' Roses to the Beatles from showing up together in the same building to receive their laurels. And we have seen cussing, sneering, and the flashing of middle fingers meant to assure both the audience and the performers themselves that their rock and roll bona fides remained intact.

The critics are right. For the most part, rock's jubilee became a dead end for the inane and monied and self-important, but in thinking about the core urges of popular music and the essential contributions of rock and roll to our world, these nights and this institution still offer a communal nexus for reflecting upon something profound that sparkles long after the thriving of the genre has passed.

Visit YouTube clips sneaked out the back door of the Rock and Roll Empire's paywall to see the speeches, tributes, and live performance mash-ups presented to an exclusive black-tie audience of music industry insiders. Watch from afar the sharp elbows and drooping jaws and smoldering aspirations of a movement that has, often in spite of itself, done more to reimagine the power and glory of ancient myth and religion than any other cultural force over the past century.

My favorite moment on these long nights of honors and self-congratulation, and maybe the consensus greatest moment if audiences were asked, is Prince taking over "While My Guitar Gently Weeps" as

Tom Petty, Jeff Lynne, and the rest of his bandmates can only step back and watch in a kind of fanlike awe.

Bob Dylan's state-mate Prince—who could reasonably be said to have metabolized and innovated the entire popular music enterprise over the course of his sterling career before collapsing in an elevator of an overdose in his purple mansion—takes the notes of the world's most famous and beloved band, the Beatles, and turns them into a wild, wordless, spiritual, ethereal, funny, and seemingly effortless expression of human possibility to gently weep just for the sake of being alive.

Here was Jimi Hendrix's shredding, Little Richard's otherworldly cool, Elvis's smirk, and James Brown's groove. Then Prince fake-fell into the audience, smiled under the brim of his hat, dropped his guitar, and walked off the stage, as peerless an outlaw as you could ever want to see.

Bob Dylan, acknowledged by the leaders of rock and roll in speeches and tributes ritually since the beginning, has done as much as anyone to carve out a path of culture and spirit where a moment like that could come to be. Like Prince, he made a revolution of the bounty of music and texts and movies he gobbled up from the artists who had come before him. Dylan's Brandoesque "What have you got?" cool repossessed the notes of his predecessors to chart something individually and extraordinarily new, while he still seemed to stay within himself. Bob Dylan has also, whether by chance, intent, or both, played the long game, arriving to the Rock and Roll Empire as its boundaries were just being established, charging it with purpose, passing through its many iterations and trends, and outliving not just its cultural moment, but many of its most important influencers, Prince included.

I'm not thinking about popular music or the world itself After Dylan (AD) because I wish for a moment that Dylan's music and persona should cease to add new surprises to what we already have. *Rough and Rowdy Ways*, *Time Out of Mind*, *Oh Mercy*, *Blood on the Tracks*, *John*

Wesley Harding, Highway 61 Revisited—these were all unexpected turns of expression that revealed how Dylan can reimagine his inventory, our inventory, with such dexterity and guts that it is safe to assume that we are still far from seeing the final link he will add to his own chain of tradition, each one gesturing in new ways to the same thing: salvation, faith, emancipation.

Popular music, like Dylan's work, is comprised of uneasy pairings: myth and commerce, majesty and vulgarity, corporatism and individualism, disruption and tradition, immediacy and timelessness, and both reverence and disregard for so much of what adds up to spiritual wisdom in the world. Somehow these tensions have served to inspire an inherently potent canon that strives for a time stamp of forever, like *Hamlet* or the Lord's Prayer.

False Prophets

One of the most sought-after Rock and Roll Hall of Fame inductors, Bruce Springsteen, who in fact inducted Bob Dylan in 1988, models both rock's naivety and its gravitas. He blessed Jackson Browne in 2004 with references to *Paradise Lost*, a fall from Eden, "proving ourselves in the eyes of God," and facilitating one's own redemption. In 2005 he cited U2's searching for "the same kind of combustible force that fueled the expansion of the universe after the big bang. You want the earth to shake and spit fire. You want the sky to split apart and for God to pour out."

As the head teacher at the Rock and Roll Sunday School—and probably also academic chair of the University of Rock and Roll based on his tour de force keynote lecture on the history of rock and roll at the South by Southwest festival in 2012—Springsteen's metaphors are borrowed from bedrock stories of humanity that were meant to explain creation when it could not be understood in any other way. The fact that he could even think, let alone perform, this way is a direct result of

Dylan's spiritual wisdom, putting these liturgies on the radio, into our heads, selling cars and undergarments, coloring films, and accompanying us at weddings and funerals in ways that might actually continue to affirm the ineffability of the meaning of life, just like the traditional religious terms Springsteen uses to describe the music he loves.

With Dylan at the age of eighty at the time of this writing and luminaries from Prince to Tom Petty, from David Bowie to Little Richard, from Aretha Franklin to Lou Reed, already joining the friends and colleagues and the "27 Club" in rock and roll heaven—what will happen to popular music AD? Will Woodstock be a battle in the Trojan War remembered in a rock and roll *Iliad* for centuries to come? Will Dylan, like Shakespeare, simply mean *Shakespeare*, part of popular knowledge for even the most casually attuned cultural observer? When the musicians and fans of Dylan's generation are gone, and their children who were raised on the nostalgia of classic rock radio even though much of it was recorded before they were five years old are gone too, who will preserve the legacy of rock and roll for whoever and whatever comes next?

Bob Dylan said from the beginning of his career and at the beginning of this book that he ain't no false prophet. He speaks in a colloquial double negative in 2020's "False Prophet," gestures to old-timey friends like Mary Lou (that heartbreaker mother of muses still breaking hearts after all these years) and also fleet-footed Hermes. Dylan's singer on the mount is part philosopher, part ego-tripper and—what did he just say?—looking for vengeance. You can look in your Bible for this one. Look all day. Only God can have vengeance.

So what does a prophecy like that even mean, man? Why bring up vengeance in a collection of songs that, for the most part, as we have already heard, thrives in its empathetic reveries, its comforting soft edges in the face of plague, old age, and finding purpose anew? I think Dylan calls down vengeance as a gesture to his legacy, but with a bit of jest in the gesture, baring his teeth toward the end of his own contributions to a line of work which acolyte Warren Zevon once told David Letterman Dylan had invented for him and so many others.

Here Dylan makes it clear that despite the genius of many musicians of his age and era—Bruce Springsteen and Van Morrison, Joni Mitchell and Neil Young, Paul McCartney and Ray Davies, Prince, Patti Smith, Stevie Wonder, the Who, the list goes on—there simply has not been anyone like Bob Dylan. He has been and meant so many different things, and is so hard to pin down, so prolific, that there really isn't a category that suits him and anyone else at the same time. Dylan is his own hall of fame, and the only nominee is him. He wants you to know it, Mr. and Mrs. Poet. And he will head-butt you with a song like "False Prophet" if you disagree.

How Do They Feel?

Yes, Bob Dylan knows it and so do I. Despite industry efforts and every variety of hard-charging achiever, there has never been a "New Dylan," because he was the right song-and-dance man at the right time—one time, one person, one product of his times that were a-changin' and the one who changed them too.

A once-in-a-generation voice is not just about talent or calling. There is a confluence of events that sets the stage for that voice. There is an almost imperceptible blurring of boundaries between the artist as a vessel and the flow of cultural content, need, use, and wanting that shapes that vessel. Dylan inhabited the myth and created it. That's what cultural figures who come once in a generation do.

The achievement of the work itself speaks for itself. Songs such as "Blowin' in the Wind" and "Knockin' on Heaven's Door" and "The Times They Are A-Changin'" will remain to play a ceremonial role for generations, hymns of our age passed down along with "Hallelujah" and "Bridge Over Troubled Water" at events public and private. Sometimes a distinguished figure like Nina Simone—some soulful singer of the future—will turn the world upside down by pouring herself into a song-vessel Dylan made, a virtuoso performance that rediscovers a composition nearly perfect for its original context, and then made almost perfect again by sheer force of will and talent for another context with another voice that Dylan probably could not have imagined himself.

So, too, a diva like Adele may find the producer, the pipes, and the moment to capture a song like "Make You Feel My Love" as a means of expressing a feeling that connects with others on a massive scale because she is the right song-and-dance woman to bring that sentiment to life when the world needs it.

And so too long after the original punks and Bob Dylan are gone from this Earth, a kid with a chip on her shoulder will bump into Dylan's performance of "Like a Rolling Stone" after the shout of "Judas!" and understand that nothing and no one can or should ever stop her from telling everyone how *she* feels being on her own. This may be a discovery that kid makes outside of the fixed maps of Spotify or YouTube, like Columbus looking for a gateway to the East and coming ashore in the Americas instead

As algorithms become more and more sophisticated in guiding our hands and ears to the content that AI-powered economic systems of control desire, that kid may need to find the equivalent source of Dylan's scouring record stores with beatniks or the occasional hootenanny down at the union hall or searching for a clear radio signal from a Shreveport, Louisiana, radio station's gospel hour in the darkness of her bedroom because the brightly lit channels of the internet will not carry such subversions ten, twenty, or thirty years from now.

Someday, someone will ask his grandfather about Public Enemy, that moment in hip-hop, and dig deep into the catalog and find Chuck D's parsing of Dylan tunes on his "Long and Whining Road," meeting the Beatles and Dylan for the first time, curious, probing, revealing something that trips his imaginative wire in a way no one could have predicted such that something lives on, a post-everything talent transfigured.

There is no answer blowing in the wind for precisely how Bob Dylan's influence will be cultivated in the future, how the art of memory will declaim or reframe him, but we could have said the same of the Bentley Boys nearly a century ago or of the anonymous troubadours who loved to sing "Lord Randal" and its antecedents of hundreds of years prior until it became "A Hard Rain's a-Gonna Fall." Dylan's impact will be like these meandering traditions and more.

Who will hear "Blind Willie McTell"'s pained reflection of a white man unable to generate an honest song to explain the roots of his country one hundred years after emancipation or one hundred years after that? What if—heaven forfend—people of color still haven't received their due a generation or three from now, or some have and some haven't? How will this song serve as a lesson that the way station of rock and roll once offered a transfer point where travelers could learn that there were people in America who knew not only that a country had died on a cross in its fatal pact with slavery, but that somehow the flood of truth in telling the tale might break the dam of resentments and violence if it was told enough?

I believe—I hope—that someone will teach, through the song "Blind Willie McTell" and others, that Bob Dylan helped break the sonic barriers of getting this message of liberation across to people the same way that the Soul Stirrers inspired him and he inspired Sam Cooke and MLK prophesied his dreams and died for them, and then eventually, finally, history became the future that it was meant to be.

Dylan's spiritual legacy will be, as Miles Davis once described as a measure of musical greatness, more about the notes he does not play than the ones he does. His musical roadmap for the soul is his riddles keeping his listeners asking more questions, transcending and producing and reproducing esoteric truths within the traditions upon which our culture is based. His testament over decades is that creative work must be contrarian, exhaustive, informed, and empathetic to consider life's purpose and practice in ways that matter.

Having launched time and again the demand of "False Prophet" that one must be the sworn enemy of the "unlived meaningless life," he puts to us, love it or leave it, the same life-and-death passion for truth Socrates swore upon before he was forced to drink poison as a penalty for his subversion. "The unexamined life is not worth living," Socrates said, no false prophet indeed.

Dylan's music guides humanity toward knowledge it needs desperately to survive in the 21st century—a repurposing of all those preceding millennia of spiritual wisdom—at a time when the old ways of man and God and law no longer sustain us, maybe even cheapen us, maybe even hold us in an ignorant grip at our peril. But the damage that these ideas do in the wrong hearts and hands does not mean that those ideas are corrupt, only that the people who corrupt them are corrupt. The masters of war who made the pawns who played before the law with the wrong rules of the game and forced God to take their side until they too were felled—these are the broken vessels rattling down the hall.

What came first, Bob Dylan or a world clamoring for him without even knowing it? I think that it was the latter, and that the need for spiritual wisdom in popular culture won't change. It will only grow. More than one hundred years ago, French sociologist Emile Durkheim wrote that "the former gods are growing old or dying, and others have not been born."[45] My hunch is that whether he is acknowledged specifically or not, Dylan's birth and bridge from old world to new will continue to serve humanity in this way.

Bob Dylan once said, "He not busy being born is busy dying." The same could be said of any person, any musician or spiritual leader, and certainly, if our place on this Earth means anything at all, the world itself. We are always renewed, always being born, and our greatest artists, like Bob Dylan, not only urge what's next into being but make room for the next set of gods and stars, ethereal and in some sense eternal reflections of both who we are and who we most want to be when we least expect it.

So much of this future is already here. Not long ago, scholar Daphne Brooks wrote eloquently in *Liner Notes for the Revolution: The Intellectual Life of Black Feminist Sound*[46] that the mythological musical age of Dylan ended when the age of Beyoncé began, she of sublime talent and messages of emancipation, a powerful Black woman commanding a world stage, innovating visual expression across media—and as a queen rather than a king, commanding that her audience think about what she has come to say from her new-world perspective and vision. This just one example of the immense opportunities of music After Dylan.

We Can Feel

Rudolf Otto, a theologian in the first part of the 20th century, posed a question Dylan would spend a career trying to answer: "How does it feel?" In *The Idea of the Holy*[47], Otto described the holiness as a feeling, "the numinous," a sense of life's essence, a space differentiated and "other" from everywhere else—a place beyond places that still affirms everywhere and every place and any direction home we might chose to go.

How does holiness feel in a world flattened by technology, a pandemic, and power and greed and corruptible seed? Music tells us.

A recent film, *Ma Rainey's Black Bottom*, quotes one of the great figures of the blues with a similar sentiment about an "it" where the blues, meaning American music and meaning America, can also be heard as the holiness Otto and Dylan both seek: "They hear it come out, but they don't know how it got there. They don't understand that's life's way of talking. You don't sing to feel better. You sing 'cause that's a way of understanding life."

Bob Dylan plays notes that describe what we cannot explain: the holy, the blues, the essence of life. This "it" is that feeling that comes from the muses to musicians, the messengers of the most powerful, transformative tool of our expressive age.

There is a kid somewhere—there are thousands who could be that kid—who will have that same urge to seek "it," to seek the holy, to know how it feels. Growing up and out of place, stuck in themselves or their family or neighborhood or their nation and yearning to be free, to connect, to feel, their pathway will not be an easy one, but it will be theirs for the taking when they are ready.

A singer may head east to go west, or maybe they will just wander for a while. As they open to what they hear in their head, the world will open as their chorus to show them how it feels to be on their own, with no direction home. There will be an echo of Bob Dylan in their voice, or maybe he will even be a soulful companion in their heart, or maybe he will be a complete unknown to them, and their voice will rightly be wholly and completely their own. They may know how Dylan animates their voice as Dylan knew that his was embodying Woody Guthrie's when he first found it. Or perhaps, in the same flow of mysteries and transfigurations Bob Dylan leans into, they will not know all the voices blending into their own unique expression. Bob Dylan will be a ghost in their machine, but a very friendly one.

One day they will be called the voice of their generation just as Bob Dylan was called the voice of his, but they will demur. They will say, come on now, I'm just a song-and-dance person, I'm just a singer. But they won't deny their talent and they will work it like no one else works it, taking that inventory passed down from Alexandria and Athens, Rome and Jerusalem, St. Louis and Liverpool and Hibbing, passed onward to Detroit or Dallas or Atlanta, reinventing those great ideas once again.

Because they will be the vessel of spiritual wisdom for their age, just as Bob Dylan was for his, they will know how it feels even as they ask us that question over and over: *How does it feel?* They, like Dylan, will not tell us how to answer this question, but in their asking, we will get the feeling that they know an answer, maybe even *the* answer—both for them and for us, us and them. In our hearing them ask us this question with such eloquence and skill with a tune from the heavens, as it has been asked by seekers and shamans and priests and sages for thousands of years—*How does it feel?*—we will, both together and on our own, feel a little better, not completely known in our not quite knowing how to respond, but certainly less alone.

And somehow, in their singing and asking, in our hearing and feeling, the more we listen, the more we will know that we all share something—a numinous, unexplainable place of blues and holiness and spiritual wisdom. As we listen to their question we will understand that the answer is the question and the question is the music that will be. Together, thanks to them, and thanks to their ancestor Bob Dylan and all those ancients, there *is* a fleeting moment when we really do know how it feels, that right place at the right time with the right voice that is a gift from somewhere beyond ourselves and within ourselves that music can bring. Then they will bow and we will cheer and all of us will thrill to knowing that we heard the same wondrous thing together.

Call it service or prophecy or worship or revelation or just plain music. Call it whatever it's called when it comes. Call it whatever you want to call it, whatever it means to you. But play it, sing it, and be observant. And be very grateful that it came for us when we needed it, and that Bob Dylan did his part so that we could do ours, and that they could do theirs, and that on and on it goes. And with that, let us say amen.

Acknowledgments

Thank you to Joy Murphy at Universal Music for her kind assistance in obtaining licenses to print excerpts of Bob Dylan's lyrics.

Kevin O'Connor and Jonathan Agin helped me find a home for this project by introducing me to Kevin Anderson. This is how I found my partners at Morgan James Publishers. Thank you, Kevin, Jonathan, and Kevin, and thank you, David Hancock, the founder of MJP, MJP's publisher Jim Howard, as well as the patient, generous, and wonderful Bonnie Rauch and the entire MJP team for professionalism, positivity, attention to detail, and execution in bringing this book to completion.

Aja Pollock, Amanda Rogers, Jennifer Safrey, and Miriam Yifrach provided editorial guidance, for which I am grateful. My thanks to Sharon Gabay for the author's photo.

Thank you to the Podfam at Pantheon Podcasts (www.Pantheon-Podcasts.com), led by Christian Swain and Peter Ferioli. I'm proud to be a part of this music-loving crew and grateful for the wide-open spaces it has offered for creating the *Bob Dylan: About Man and God and Law* podcast (www.mangodlaw.com), where I cultivated much of what I wanted to say in the book. Christian's brilliant Rock N Roll Archaeology podcast is an inspiration and highly recommended to all.

Love and thanks to: Nicholas Diamand and Laura Bailyn for legal advice and kindness; Eyal Regev, Alec Thomson, Ruth Cummings,

Nigel Savage, Matt Coen, and Marco Greenberg for friendship and encouragement; my sister, Jane, my father, Joseph, and my mother and stepfather, Gail and George, music lovers all; and to my cuz, Jonathan Torop, my rock.

I know that Dave Bry of blessed memory offered whatever heaven would allow of his edits, musical knowledge, and all-hours humor from somewhere, always treasured. Rami Wernik was also watching as I stumbled bleary-eyed to my final deadlines for the book, cheering me on. Here's to you both, Rami and Dave, brothers gone too soon.

I offer thanks to Marty Werber and the board of the Fuchsberg Jerusalem Center (www.fuchsbergcenter.org), where I am honored to serve as CEO, for their profound support of my writing this book. I also thank my colleagues at FJC, especially Joshua Halickman, David Keren, and Tamara Fine Skversky, who have been exceedingly patient and helpful despite the interruptions in my work schedule that writing has required.

Thank you to my book buddy Cheryll Bellamy for an enthusiastic reading of an early draft and good vibes always. Thank you, Halley Moore, whose amazingly wise and timely suggestions and edits along with her warm encouragement were profoundly, formatively essential to this work.

And then there's my dear friend, David Billotti. He read every word of this book more than once. Some of those words are his, many of the best ones in fact. David blessed me with insight, patience, kindness, incredibly deep and diverse knowledge and conversation about music and culture, and life-saving humor and advice. Thank you, David. Visit www.dylansabbath.com to join our interfaith project celebrating Bob Dylan, empathy, and enlightenment with people and communities around the world in May 2022.

This book is dedicated to my children, who have listened to more Bob Dylan songs than most. Remember that time we heard "See You

Later Allen Ginsberg" driving in Twinkle from New York to Boston? You just could not believe that Dylan could laugh like that. We must have listened to that song ten times in a row, all of us laughing right along. You know how much this music means to me, but nothing will ever mean as much to me as you. May God bless and keep you always. I love you so much.

And finally, boundless thanks to Bob Dylan—for a lifetime of music, for being there no matter who I was or where I was bound, and for always knowing how it feels.

About the Author

Stephen Daniel Arnoff has contributed to anthologies on Bob Dylan (*Dylan at Play*) and Bruce Springsteen (*Reading the Boss*) and hosts Bob Dylan: About Man and God and Law on the Pantheon Podcast Network. A writer, musician, and teacher, he lives in Jerusalem, where he is CEO of the Fuchsberg Jerusalem Center. Find out more at www.mangodlaw.com.

Bob Dylan Lyrics: Copyright Information

"Absolutely Sweet Marie." Written by Bob Dylan. © Universal Tunes. All rights reserved. International copyright secured. Reprinted by permission.

"A Hard Rain's a-Gonna Fall." Written by Bob Dylan. © Universal Tunes. All rights reserved. International copyright secured. Reprinted by permission.

"Ain't Talkin'." Written by Bob Dylan. © Universal Tunes. All rights reserved. International copyright secured. Reprinted by permission.

"Ballad of a Thin Man." Written by Bob Dylan. © Universal Tunes. All rights reserved. International copyright secured. Reprinted by permission.

"Blind Willie McTell." Written by Bob Dylan. © Universal Tunes. All rights reserved. International copyright secured. Reprinted by permission.

"Blowin' in the Wind." Written by Bob Dylan. © Universal Tunes. All rights reserved. International copyright secured. Reprinted by permission.

"Bob Dylan's 115th Dream." Written by Bob Dylan. © Universal Tunes. All rights reserved. International copyright secured. Reprinted by permission.

"Brownsville Girl." Written by Bob Dylan. © Universal Tunes. All rights reserved. International copyright secured. Reprinted by permission.

"Death Is Not the End." Written by Bob Dylan. © Universal Tunes. All rights reserved. International copyright secured. Reprinted by permission.

"Desolation Row." Written by Bob Dylan. © Universal Tunes. All rights reserved. International copyright secured. Reprinted by permission.

"Every Grain of Sand." Written by Bob Dylan. © Universal Tunes. All rights reserved. International copyright secured. Reprinted by permission.

"False Prophet." Written by Bob Dylan. © Universal Tunes. All rights reserved. International copyright secured. Reprinted by permission.

Endnotes

1   Chris Smith, *101 Albums that Changed Popular Music* (Oxford: Oxford University Press, 2009), 31.

2   "*Rolling Stone*'s 100 Greatest Singers of All Time," *Rolling Stone*, December 3, 2010, accessed May 8, 2021, www.rollingstone.com/music/music-lists/100-greatest-singers-of-all-time-147019/.

3   Nat Hentoff, "A Candid Conversation with the Iconoclastic Idol of the Folk-Rock Set," *Playboy*, February 1966, 82.

4   Greil Marcus, *Invisible Republic: Bob Dylan's Basement Tapes* (New York: Henry Holt and Company, Inc., 1997), xviii.

5   Ellen Willis, *Out of the Vinyl Deeps: Ellen Willis on Rock and Roll* (Minneapolis: University of Minnesota Press, 2011), 15.

6   Emile Durkheim, *The Elementary Forms of Religious Life* (New York: Free Press, 1995), 421.

7   Jonathan I. Israel, *Radical Enlightenment: Philosophy and the Making of Modernity 1650–1750* (London: Oxford University Press, 2001), 3.

8   Charles Taylor, *A Secular Age* (Cambridge: Harvard University Press, 2007), 25.

9   Ibid.,152.

10   Robert Pattison, *The Triumph of Vulgarity: Rock Music in the Mirror of Romanticism* (London: Oxford University Press, 1987), 88.

11   Ibid., xi.

12   Ibid., xii.

13   Max Weber, *The Protestant Ethic and the Spirit of Capitalism* (London: Routledge Classics, 2001), 146.

14   Charles Kaiser, "The Unlikely, Lifesaving Queerness of Bob Dylan," *Slate*, May 25, 2021, https://slate.com/human-interest/2021/05/bob-dylan-queer-icon-allen-ginsberg.html.

15   Plato, *Symposium* (Indianapolis, IN: Hackett Publishing Company, 1989), 27.

16   Sigmund Freud, *Civilization and Its Discontents* (New York: W. W. Norton, 1962), 2.

17   Esther Perel, "Building Resilient Relationships," interview with Manoush Zomorodi, *TED Radio Hour*, September 11, 2020, www.npr.org/2020/09/10/911392320/esther-perel-building-resilient-relationships.

18   Hannah Arendt, *Love and Saint Augustine* (Chicago: University of Chicago Press, 1998), 15.

19   Oscar Wilde, *De Profundis*, accessed May 8, 2021, www.gutenberg.org/files/921/921-h/921-h.htm.

20   "Raeben, Norman," *The Bob Dylan Who's Who*, on ExpectingRain.com, accessed May 8, 2021, expectingrain.com/dok/who/r/raebennorman.html.

21   Saint Augustine, *Confessions*, 12:28.

22   Ibid., 8:28.

23   Ibid., 8:29.

24   Richard Thomas, *Why Dylan Matters* (New York: HarperCollins*Publishers*, 2017).

25   Adam Cohen, "Adam Cohen Talks to Janice Forsyth About His Father Leonard Cohen's Posthumous Album," interview by Janice Forsyth, *The Afternoon Show*, November 11, 2019, www.bbc.co.uk/programmes/p07tnpnk.

26   Leonard Cohen, *The Book of Longing* (Toronto: McClelland & Stewart, 2006), 4.

27   Plato, *Cratylus* 402a = A6.

28   Dante Alighieri, trans. Allen Mandelbaum, *Digital Dante*, accessed May 25, 2021, https://digitaldante.columbia.edu/dante/divine-comedy/inferno/inferno-1/.

29   Marcus, *Invisible Republic*, 139-143.

30   Jonathan Cott, *Bob Dylan: The Essential Interviews* (New York: Simon and Schuster, 2007), 452.

31   Christopher Ricks, *Dylan's Vision of Sin* (New York: Ecco, 2003), 329-344.

[32]   Jenny Ledeen, *Prophecy in the Christian Era* (St. Louis, MO: Peaceberry Press of Webster Groves, 1995).

[33]   Suzanne Vega, "The Ballad of Henry Timrod," *New York Times*, September 17, 2006, www.nytimes.com/2006/09/17/opinion/17vega.html.

[34]   "He's a Plagiarist, and His Name and Voice Are Fake," *Pop and Hiss: The Los Angeles Times Music Blog*, accessed May 8, 2021, https://latimesblogs.latimes.com/music_blog/2010/04/joni-mitchell-on-bob-dylan-hes-a-plagiarist-his-name-is-fake-his-voice-is-fake.html.

[35]   Jonathan Lethem, "The Ecstasy of Influence," *Harper's Magazine*, February 2007, https://harpers.org/archive/2007/02/the-ecstasy-of-influence/.

[36]   Scott Warmuth, "Bob Dylan's Secret Answer Record: The Uncle John Connection," *Goon Talk* (blog), December 12, 2015, http://swarmuth.blogspot.com/2015/12/bob-dylans-secret-answer-record-uncle.html.

[37]   John Cohen, liner notes for *Modern Times* by the New Lost City Ramblers, Folkways Records, FTS 31027, 1968, vinyl LP.

[38]   Mary Carruthers, *The Book of Memory: A Study of Memory in Medieval Culture* (Cambridge: Cambridge University Press, 1990), 260.

[39]   Brian Hinton, *Both Sides Now* (London: Sanctuary Publishing Ltd, 1996), 76–77.

[40]   Bob Dylan, *Chronicles: Volume One* (New York: Simon and Schuster, 2004), 84–86.

[41]   Clinton Heylin, *Behind the Shades: The 20th Anniversary Edition* (London: Faber and Faber, 2011), 741.

[42]   Ricks, *Dylan's Vision of Sin*, 6.

[43]   Heylin, *Behind the Shades*, 791.

[44]   Moshe Idel, *New Perspectives* (New Haven: Yale University Press, 1990).

[45]   Durkheim, *Elementary Forms*, 475.

[46]   Daphne A. Brooks, *Liner Notes for the Revolution: The Intellectual of Black Feminist Sound* (Cambridge, Massachusetts: The Belknap Press of Harveard University Press, 2021), 432–445.

[47]   Rudolf Otto, *The Idea of the Holy* (Oxford: Oxford University Press, 1958).

A free ebook edition
is available with the
purchase of this book.

To claim your free ebook edition:

1. Visit MorganJamesBOGO.com
2. Sign your name CLEARLY in the space
3. Complete the form and submit a photo of the entire copyright page
4. You or your friend can download the ebook to your preferred device

Print & Digital Together Forever.

Snap a photo   Free ebook   Read anywhere

CPSIA information can be obtained
at www.ICGtesting.com
Printed in the USA
JSHW041308070422
24710JS00001B/1